Praise for
Engaging the Hearts and Minds of All Your Employees

"Ignite Passionate Performance! This breakthrough book absolutely nails what it takes to connect with your customers and provide passionate service. Engaged employees are the fuel that will power your future success."

David Cottrell
CEO, CornerStone Leadership Institute,
Author of *Monday Morning Leadership* and
Monday Morning Choices

"This practical guide delivers the right message at a critical time . . . engage your people! It's a swift read and provides fresh, new insights. Colan's framework enables leaders to see the person behind the employee as the first step to igniting Passionate Performance. It's the secret sauce to today's leading organizations."

Jim Thyen
President and CEO, Kimball International

"Colan has an ability to accentuate what leaders are already doing well, while helping them apply new and different techniques for leading more effectively. *Engaging the Hearts and Minds* emphasizes meeting both intellectual and emotional needs of associates. The passionate performance model helped to successfully prepare our managers to engage their teams as we executed our strategy."

Sara E. Lee
Vice President, Human Resources
Pier 1 Imports

"A quick and actionable read! Colan is true to form with clear insights and practical tools for engaging your team. A fully engaged team sets an organization apart in any market—good or bad. This book should be read by every leader who wants to conquer the competition."

Stephen Mansfield
President and CEO
Methodist Health System

"In *Engaging the Hearts and Minds*, Colan gives us a simple framework and a practical guide. The result is convincing—an advantage that our competitors will find very difficult to replicate. A quick read that can make a big difference."

Steven Leven
Former Senior Vice President
Worldwide Human Resources
Texas Instruments

"Colan not only artfully writes about engaging the hearts and minds of our team, but he also engages the reader's heart and mind in doing so. He brings to life the complex concept of employee engagement with powerful tools that challenge the mind and compelling illustrations that inspire the heart. You will experience *passionate performance* while you learn about it!"

Chris Widener
Bestselling Author, *The Art of Influence*

"I bought a copy of your latest book *Engaging the Hearts and Minds of All Your Employees* last Friday, and was so mesmerized by your content and passionate performance model that I had to read it in one sitting. Your concepts resonated so strongly with me and provided much insight into the dissatisfaction and disengagement I've seen and experienced in the workplace."

Pauline L. Perreault
Jump Outta Bed (J.O.B.)
Workplace Strategies

"A lot of companies have hands and feet coming to work every day . . . a lot of average companies. *Engaging the Hearts and Minds* describes how to turn hands and feet into minds and hearts—the combination that it takes to win in today's business environment."

Dave Loeser
Senior Vice President
Worldwide Human Resources, Unisys

"Once again, Colan's simple and direct message reminds us of the employee engagement principles we have all experienced in our careers, but tend to forget to execute."

Joe Bosch
Former Chief People Officer
Pizza Hut and DirecTV

"This rapid-read guide book will help everyone grow! From first-time supervisors to the most seasoned executives. It provides clear, simple techniques for winning the minds and hearts of your workforce. A must read."

Jeff Reeves
Former Sr. Vice President
Human Resources, Wal-Mart and Allianz

"A great book and dead-on with what we're experiencing. Colan's practical advice has unleashed the power of full engagement in our company. Our people and their passion have turned an ordinary business of moving molecules through a cold, steel pipeline into an extraordinary story of service and customer satisfaction."

Barry E. Davis
Chairman and CEO, EnLink Midstream

"We want and need for our customers to 'love' us because they do have alternatives. To achieve this, our team members must be fully engaged. This book reminds us of what is really important."

Mark Blinn
CEO, Flowserve

"*Engaging the Hearts and Minds* is a powerful and practical reminder that our primary job as a leader (of a department, of a home, of a company) is to engage all of a person. Colan's model not only provides us with a compass for where we want to go, but then provides specific, simple, and actionable steps to begin the journey. It's a winner!"

Lisa Lapiska
Vice President, People Improvement, Fossil

"I read *Engaging the Hearts and Minds* last night. It is a superb piece of work. In my several decades of business management in corporate America, I used many of the ideas and techniques that you describe. They really worked!

I just did not have the imagination or the wit to write a book about it. This book is worth far more than the purchase price to the right person, at the right time, with the right application."

Robert J. Potter, PhD
Former Senior Executive
Nortel, International Harvest, and Xerox

"Colan is a master communicator. In this book, he has woven practical insights and engaging stories for engaging leaders to create immediate impact."

Vince Poscente
New York Times Bestselling Author of
The Age of Speed

ENGAGING

the

HEARTS

and

MINDS

of all your

EMPLOYEES

Other books by Lee J. Colan:

- Stick with It: Mastering the Art of Adherence

- The 5 Coaching Habits of Excellent Leaders: How to Create the Reliability Advantage for Your Team

- Orchestrating Attitude: Getting the Best from Yourself and Others

- 107 Ways to Stick to It

- 7 Moments...That Define Excellent Leaders

- Leadership Matters: Daily Insights to Inspire Extraordinary Results

- Power Exchange: Boosting Accountability and Performance in Today's Workforce

- Inspire! Connecting with Students to Make a Difference

- The Nature of Excellence

- Winners Always Quit: Seven Pretty Good Habits You Can Swap for Really Great Results

ENGAGING
the
HEARTS
and
MINDS
of all your
EMPLOYEES

How to Ignite Passionate Performance
for Better Business Results

Lee J. Colan, PhD

New York   Chicago   San Francisco   Athens   London   Madrid
Mexico City   Milan   New Delhi   Singapore   Sydney   Toronto

1 2 3 4 5 6 7 8 9   QFR   22 21 20 19 18 17

ISBN   978-1-260-11691-5
MHID   1-260-11691-3

e-ISBN 978-0-07-160216-7
e-MHID   0-07-160216-X

This publication is designed to provide accurate and authoritative information in
regard to the subject matter covered. It is sold with the understanding that the publisher is not engaged in rendering legal, accounting, or other professional service. If
legal advice or other expert assistance is required, the services of a competent professional person should be sought.
—From a Declaration of Principles Jointly Adopted by a Committee of the American
Bar Association and a Committee of Publishers and Associations

McGraw-Hill Education books are available at special quantity discounts to use as
premiums and sales promotions, or for use in corporate training programs. To contact a representative, please visit the Contact Us page at www.mhprofessional.com.

CONTENTS

FOREWORD TO THE PAPERBACK EDITION

Just exactly what is employee "engagement"? In this book, which you now hold in your hands, Lee Colan defines three different types of employees:

1. *Engaged* employees love their work and look forward to it every day.

2. *Disengaged* employees "punch the clock," but are not involved in the work.

3. *Actively disengaged* employees don't like their work and let it be known throughout the workplace.

Lee's definitions are spot-on, and the number of employees on your team who fall into each of these categories will factor greatly in determining how successful or unsuccessful your team and your business will be. I'll bet you already know which category you want your employees to fall into and whether or not they fall into that category.

In *Engaging the Hearts and Minds of All Your Employees,* Lee teaches leaders how to engage their employees and how they can achieve 100 percent commitment from their teams. In my favorite part of the book, Lee relates a statement by the great Peter Drucker to engagement. In this profound statement, Peter advised leaders to, "Accept the fact that we have to treat almost anybody as a volunteer." This statement strikes a chord because there is quite a distinction between what Drucker advised and the way many leaders perceive their employees. Many leaders treat their employees as cogs in the wheel. As a result, there is little engagement, if any, and more often than not, active disengagement. The underlying belief of this type of leader is that, because employees are being compensated for their work, they should be able to do their work and enjoy it. Unfortunately, this is not the case.

The good news is that you can follow Lee's road map to engage the hearts and minds of your employees. He skillfully simplifies the art of engagement into actionable steps any leader can take. Your team will not only be more fully engaged, they will also act like owners of the business and deliver better service and business results. The bonus is that they will be excited and inspired to come to work every day!

Life is good.

Marshall Goldsmith
The *Thinkers 50* #1 Leadership Thinker
in the World

INTRODUCTION

As the pace of business quickens and competition stiffens, organizations and their leaders continue to ask, "How can we achieve a *significant and sustainable* competitive advantage?"

Far removed from the simple models of the past, today's businesses must consider a dizzying variety of factors to ensure their competitiveness. Factors like product design, technology, and distribution channels have to be maximized just to maintain market share. The time-honored "four Ps of marketing"—product, price, promotion and placement—have become less important today than factors like agility, creativity, supply chain efficiency, and Internet visibility and access. As complexity continues to infiltrate every aspect of business, a fifth P—people—has become increasingly important as a competitive factor.

As complexity continues to infiltrate every aspect of business, a fifth P—people—has become increasingly important as a competitive factor.

Consider the last time you interacted with a sales representative, whether at a retail store or on the telephone. More than likely, your decision to buy, not to buy, or even to buy more than you had planned was influenced by how engaging the representative was. Did he or she greet you promptly, ask about your needs, and offer to help you meet your needs? Did he or she solve a problem for you, make an observation about you, find a topic of common interest for discussion, and so on. In addition, 70 percent of the U.S. gross domestic product comes from services and information, generated and delivered by *people*.[1]

Bottom line: people buy from people, not from companies. This means that your people—and their performance— are your organization's defining, competitive advantage.

U.S. workers, or workers in any country for that matter, come in three varieties:

- *Engaged employees:* They love what they are doing, and they look forward to coming to work. They are passionate about what they do, feel that they are an important part of the big picture and that their energy and innovation make their companies not only successful but competitive, as well.

- *Disengaged employees:* They are punching the clock, but if you look into their eyes, you'll find that their hearts and minds are elsewhere. They're at work, most of the time, but they left their energy and their passion at home.

- *Actively disengaged employees:* These employees are not only just putting in their time and feeling unhappy about being there, but they're also spreading the gloom as they demonstrate how much they're unhappy with their boss, coworkers, or the company in general. While their engaged counterparts are working passionately, the actively disengaged are feverishly sabotaging every positive accomplishment.[2]

When people are fully engaged in their work and have a deep connection with what they do, they deliver "Passionate Performance." Passionate Performers demonstrate a strong, sustained intellectual and emotional attachment to their work.

What percentage of employees do you think are engaged?

According to an extensive survey conducted by the Gallup organization, 74 percent of employees are either indifferent to their work or actively disengaged. This leaves 26 percent

> **Passionate Performers demonstrate a strong, sustained intellectual and emotional attachment to their work.**

of employees who are engaged. The actively disengaged group is characterized as employees intentionally acting in ways that negatively affect their organizations.[3]

The Business Case for Engagement

Let's turn our focus to Passionate Performance—the main reason you have satisfied customers and, ultimately, the basis for your team's success.

Research by Hewitt Associates, the human resources outsourcing and consulting firm, indicated that companies with double-digit growth:

- Had senior leaders who were 25 percent more engaged than their employees and more engaged than leaders in single-digit growth organizations.

- Were passionate about creating a positive work environment and culture.

- Instilled pride and engendered a growth mindset in their employees.

- Provided greater opportunities for support and development.[4]

By emphasizing employee engagement, the leadership of Molson Coors Brewing Company was able to save $1,721,760 in safety costs in 2002. A survey that same year found engaged employees to be five times less likely to be involved in an accident at work and seven times less likely to have a lost-time safety incident than their disengaged counterparts.[5]

In a 2007 study, two professors from Manchester Business School in the United Kingdom interviewed 4,700 customers and employees of 63 businesses. At the conclusion of their study, one thing was clear—**companies were more likely to be growing if employee satisfaction exceeded customer satisfaction.**[6]

Additional research found that employee and customer views are usually similar, indicating that employees' attitudes strongly influence those of the customers. As a result, year-on-year sales growth shows that the more the employees' view of the company outshines the customers', the more the sales grow. Why? Because employees' views tend to transfer to customers.

Nordstrom's legendary customer service is a perfect example. Its service is epitomized by the story of the Nordstrom employee who allowed an unhappy elderly customer to return a set of automobile tires for a refund, even though Nordstrom is a high-fashion retailer that doesn't sell tires![7] All in the name of trying to deliver superb service. Would you go back to Nordstrom's if this happened to you?

The Customer Value Chain

Think of the times you've gone shopping or to a restaurant and dealt with people who were visibly happy to be in their jobs—and to have the opportunity to serve you. Their words were from their hearts, rather than the mandatory, "Can I help you?" They probably surprised you with the extra effort and thoughtfulness they displayed in satisfying your particular needs, answering your questions, or offering suggestions. They actually seemed delighted to do it!

How did you feel when you left these businesses? Did you buy more and did you spend more time than you initially planned? Are you likely to return? Have you recommended these businesses to friends?

If you answered yes to at least one of these questions, you began a value chain that was based on employees who were actively engaged.

If you search the Internet for the term "engaged employees," you'll come up with about 2 million hits including many examples. Most of these examples are of companies

> **If you search the Internet for the term "engaged employees," you'll come up with about 2 million hits including many examples. Most of these examples are of companies where employees are actively engaged. Interestingly, they are the same companies known for superior service.**

where employees are actively engaged. Interestingly, they are the same companies known for superior service such as Walt Disney, Audi, and GE.

The philosophy of these companies centers around the idea that if employees are happy, they'll be engaged, they'll deliver Passionate Performance, and their customers will be happy too. In other words, they understand the customer value chain.

Here's the reality. Some people are naturally engaged in their work. They are energized and positive, and they consistently deliver Passionate Performance. Even those who are not as energized or passionate can be led to deliver Passionate Performance. Remember, leaders are the first link in the customer value chain. Engaging leaders invest their time and

> **Leaders are the first link in the customer value chain.**

energy into their teams because they know that engaged employees are more likely to:

- Stay with the organization.

- Perform at high levels.

- Influence others to perform well.

- Promote the organization externally.

- Deliver unparalleled customer service.

These outcomes illustrate the customer value chain, which is illustrated below.

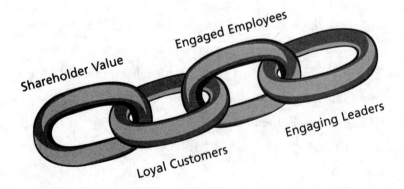

The Customer Value Chain

The customer value chain starts with an engaging leader. Engaging leaders ignite a fully engaged worker. Fully engaged workers create loyal customers. We know that gaining additional business from an existing customer is five times less expensive than acquiring a new customer. A loyal customer base is the grand slam of business. It creates higher profit margins and better returns for shareholders. There are no shortcuts in the customer value chain. We can't just hope for more loyal customers. We can't just hire engaged employees and stop there; **hiring effectively is necessary but is not sufficient to build an engaged team.**

With enough time and resources, your competitors might be able to replicate your products, distribution channels, and technology. However, they will not be able to easily duplicate Passionate Performance. **Passionate Performance creates a rock-solid wall of differentiation between you and the rest of the pack**.

Tom Peters, the renowned management guru and author once said, "If your company is going to put customers first, then you must put employees more first."[8] That's because your employees are a key link in the customer value chain.

Maximizing Your ROIT

This book provides 12 practical strategies to ignite Passionate Performance in your team. Applying these strategies will begin a powerful and self-reinforcing cycle that builds value within your team and reaches out to your customers and shareholders.

I hope you will use these strategies to inspire your own heart and mind with ideas that help you bring out Passionate Performance in every member of your team!

To maximize your ROIT—return on invested time—here are a few tips on how to use this book. The key is to *interact with this book* by:

- Underlining or highlighting points that help you.

- Taking time to work through the "Pulse Points" (sidebars sprinkled throughout the book that include exercises, actionable tips, or reflection questions).

- Reflecting on each chapter and writing down one simple action you can take to improve. Look for the heading "Fulfilling the Need" at the end of some chapters.

- Taking the two-part Passionate Performance leadership profile assessment in the Appendix to help you prioritize which areas will help you most quickly elevate your leadership skills.

Read, enjoy, apply, and engage!

PART I

Getting Your Head (and Your Heart) around Engagement

The Anatomy of Passionate Performance

Management guru Peter Drucker advises leaders to, "Accept the fact that we have to treat almost anybody as a volunteer."[9] When you see this concept—employees as volunteers—it reminds you as a leader of your responsibility to continually engage your people.

The key to turning volunteers into "owners" is found within the hearts and minds of your employees. When their basic human needs are fulfilled, you can achieve full engagement with a simple but powerful formula: When my needs are fulfilled, I am engaged and I perform at my peak ability.

When employees' needs are met, they will be motivated to help those who meet their needs. When their needs are

> **When my needs are fulfilled, I am engaged and I perform at my peak ability.**

not met, they become frustrated, out of control, unfocused, and disconnected—in a word, disengaged.

We all have these basic human needs, and they have remained the same, in spite of the tumultuous changes of today's business environment. Yes, times have changed, our world has changed, and the ways we do business have changed, but people have not changed.

To become a more engaging leader, make it a priority to get to know your employees. By knowing who they are, as people, you can better fulfill their needs to keep them fully engaged. If you can see your employees as people, you can identify six basic needs—three emotional and three intellectual are listed here.

Six Basic Needs of Employees

Intellectual (Mind) Needs	Emotional (Heart) Needs
Achievement	Purpose
Autonomy	Intimacy
Mastery	Appreciation

As you study these needs, you'll see that they are interdependent. For example, to engage the hearts of your employees, you'll need to fulfill all three of the emotional needs. And the same is true to engage their minds; you'll need to fulfill all of their intellectual needs.

> **Engaged minds build employee performance, and engaged hearts ignite employees' passion.**

Therefore, achieving Passionate Performance is a two-sided challenge: emotional and intellectual. To be successful, you must be able to engage the hearts and the minds of your employees.

In encouraging Passionate Performance, you'll find that the heart and mind must work together. Engaged minds build employee performance, and engaged hearts ignite employees' passion.

Performance without passion tends to falter during tough times or in the face of challenges that require sacrifice, significant extra effort, or unusually creative solutions. Conversely, passion without performance results in watered-down and unfocused efforts. The diagram on page 16 illustrates these concepts.

Some people are naturally wired to give everything they can to do their jobs and to help the business grow, wherever they are. These people are not the rule. In fact, the majority of employees require skilled leaders who nurture and guide them along, welcoming their ideas, asking for their feedback, and making them feel valued. Engaging leaders ultimately help their employees see and realize their potential. The real competitor for each of us, individually, is our own potential.

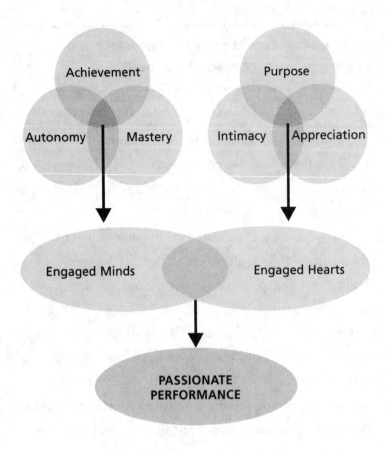

This critical leadership role reminds me of a powerful line from a favorite movie of mine, *The Lion King*. After Simba has walked away from the kingdom his father, Mufasa, left behind, he hears his father's thundering voice beckon, "Simba, you are more than what you have become."

A close look at great companies reveals a common theme: They have leaders who engage the hearts and minds of their employees and, therefore, are able to evoke Passionate Performance from their teams.

> *"Empty pockets never held anyone back. Only empty heads and empty hearts can do that."*
>
> —NORMAN VINCENT PEALE

You've just walked through the door of your office? What's happening?

Do you hear the excitement and feel the rhythm of people who love what they do and are happy to be there? Or are you greeted by a down-spirited, lifeless environment where folks are gathered but only in body because their minds and hearts are elsewhere?

As you look around, do you see people who are actually enjoying what they do? Is anyone "on fire"? Anyone excited about a project or a specific challenge? Are people loving Mondays and hating Fridays? If you've been greeted by a humdrum vibe, chances are there's no passion.

Remember the Gallup poll and the actively disengaged employees? The Gallup organization, over a period of three years, surveyed more than 1.5 million workers, and, according to the Gallup research found that "disengaged" workers tend to be significantly less productive, are less loyal to their companies, less satisfied with their personal lives, and more stressed and insecure about their work than their "engaged" counterparts.[10]

Gallup also found that actively disengaged employees miss an average of 3.5 days per year more than other workers, or, 86.5 million total days each year.[11]

So how do you know if your employees are demonstrating Passionate Performance? The test is simple. First, you'll feel their enthusiasm and see their results. Your team will have more fun creating better outcomes. Team members will be fully present at work, in the moment, in the flow.

Passionate Performance also looks like people performing at higher levels and being motivated to do more. They'll feel like kids in a candy store.

How often have you heard someone say, "I can't believe they pay me to do this"? That's what engaged people say as they deliver Passionate Performance. Why? Because their work actually feels like play.

There are organizations that have taken this element of passion and play and embedded it into their culture.

From its founding, Southwest Airlines' former CEO Herb Kelleher created a culture of fun that began with new employees' orientation. New hires walked into a room filled with balloons, confetti scattered over the tables, bright, colorful posters on the walls, and music blaring.

Lorraine Grubbs-West, a Southwest employee for two decades, vividly remembered her first day on the job: "It was hard not to be excited. There were games and several videos, including one that showed various employees describing their departmental functions in rap rhythms, capped off by none other than the CEO, introduced as 'chairman and chief DJ.'"

Kelleher appeared, dancing and rapping, "My name is Herb, Big Daddyo. You all know me. I run the show! But, without your help, there'd be no love . . . on the ground or in the air above."

Grubbs-West said that there also were serious messages offered during the orientation, but as soon as new employees walked through the door of Southwest Airlines, Kelleher and his team gave them reason to believe they had found a home away from home. "We wanted to provide a bonding experience as quickly as possible so they would begin embracing the Southwest Airlines culture," Grubbs-West said.

If you have ever flown on Southwest, you've probably seen evidence of the culture Kelleher created. On most flights, Southwest employees seem to really like what they do. They're passionate about your comfort and your safety—and their job is to have fun serving you. But Kelleher knew, like many polls show, that most employees tend to be less engaged the longer they're with the company. So to combat the inevitable loss of interest and loss of focus, this innovative CEO maintained the fun of orientation throughout the years as his company grew.

With a consistent environment that emphasized passenger safety, personal development, and fun too, Kelleher's vision was carried beyond the walls of the corporation's headquarters, into every airport Southwest serves and every flight that takes off from a Southwest ramp. It even reaches the company's passengers.[12] You can see the customer value chain at work when you watch Southwest employees interact with their customers.

The Google Corporation is another company where employees love coming to work and where Passionate Performance is the rule rather than the exception.

Cofounder Larry Page explained that the goal of every worker who comes through the door was creating the perfect search engine for the Internet. "The perfect search engine," said Page, "would understand exactly what you mean and give back exactly what you want."

Though acknowledged as the world's leading search technology company, Google's goal is to provide an even higher level of service to all those who seek information, whether they're at a desk in Boston, driving through Bonn, or strolling in Bangkok.

When named "America's Best New Company to Work For" by *Fortune* magazine, Google pulled back the curtain to reveal a campus where beach volleyball is an option, as are video games, roller hockey in the parking lot, and Foosball. It's a company that offers free cafeterias and snack rooms where new Google employees, called "nooglers," are all predicted to put on the "Google 15" (as in pounds) their first months on the job.

In a letter to prospective stockholders before its 2004 IPO, Google founders Page and Sergey Brin wrote: "Google is not a conventional company. We do not intend to become one."[13]

But Passionate Performance is *not* just about having fun with zany orientations, regular parties, Foosball tables in the break room, and concerts in the company parking lot. Remember, Passionate Performance is defined as strong, sustained intellectual and emotional attachment to one's work. **The way Passionate Performance can be ignited in your team can be as unique as your team's culture.** We tend to think of the fun loving companies when we envision Passionate Performance—Starbucks, Google, and Southwest Airlines. However, Passionate Performance is about passion *and* performance; other firms like Texas Instruments, NASA, The Container Store, TD Industries, and Crosstex Energy Services have found their unique balance between results and relationships to ignite passionately performing cultures. It's easy to focus on the passion side of Passionate Performance,

---

Passionate Performance is about passion *and* performance.

but those companies that have ignited its flame understand that it requires a dual focus-on passion for work *and* performance toward goals.

Can you remember a job or a time in your career when you felt that you worked for a great company and that your job felt like play rather than work? Maybe that feeling came when you worked on a special project where everything came together perfectly or, it could have been a team you were on where everyone did what was best for the team, thus creating a rare synergy.

Most of us can remember a work situation in which we felt that the best of our skills and talents flowed easily and naturally—and where our efforts made a real difference. Undoubtedly this was a unique experience that left us feeling special and satisfied—no, euphoric—with the results we were able to achieve. It may have been a lot of hard work, but we frequently describe it as "fun." That's because our hearts and minds were fully engaged.

Kenneth Freeman, the founding chairman and CEO of Quest Diagnostics, started from square one. When Freeman took the helm in 1996, the laboratory, which had been hastily cobbled together, was having problems with the government because of Medicare billing. There were also disgruntled customers and unhappy employees. Many of the employees were unsure of the name of their employer and referred to the company by its name before it had been acquired by another company.

Under Freeman's leadership Quest Diagnostics went from chaos to the largest medical testing firm in the world. How did he do it? "We had to get the hearts and minds of the employees—give them something to believe in, to help them understand whom they were working for, to understand their role, to take ownership for what they had to get done, and to feel excitement about what the company could become," said Freeman shortly before he handed the company's reins to his successor in 2004.[14]

I Quit, but Forgot to Tell You

Most people initially begin their jobs as engaged employees. They come to work wanting to give 110 percent. They're passionate about what they're doing and want to become a significant part of the organization. Effectively selecting engaged employees is necessary but not sufficient to achieve Passionate Performance. Even the most engaged employees can have their passion for work diffused if their leader doesn't know how to elicit Passionate Performance.

Our world of work is largely influenced by our direct leader. If I work in a crummy place but my boss is terrific, then I feel good about work and give everything I have to my team. On the contrary, I might work for a world-class organization, but my boss is not so hot. As hard as I might try, it becomes very difficult for me to give 110 percent to the team. Bottom line: We work for people, not companies . . . and employees generally leave people, not companies.

> **We work for people, not companies.**

As a leader, the challenge is that an employee departure is only the most visible and final phase of disengagement. It's a gradual process. It's more like a dimmer switch than an on-off switch that regulates our engagement. The danger in this gradual process is the interim phases—the ones I call, "I quit but forgot to tell you." It's there where disengagement is a silent killer, a cancer that is growing under the skin of your team.

I remember a retail client who experienced first-hand the silent killer nature of disengagement. It revolved around a high-performing region. This region was numero uno among eight regions for three straight years. One quarter, it dropped to number two. The regional leader assumed that it was an anomaly and waited for the next quarter. Second again. With three years at the top slot the leader figured, "Well, every good run comes to an end." The next quarter down, to third place. Now it was time to really dig in and figure out what was going on. After two more quarters of slicing and dicing numbers, he was not much closer to the root cause of fall of this region. While he spent time trying to figure out what the problem was, the region had slipped to eighth place—the bottom of the barrel!

Finally, after talking with employees at every level, the cause was revealed. Over a year earlier, one of the store leaders had begun down the path of disengagement—he did not feel that retail was a good fit for him. But like most people, did not initiate a discussion about a mutually beneficial change. He just stayed there and festered. Over time, his attitude filtered throughout his store and was ultimately felt by the store's customers who did not return. But it did not stop there. Since this particular store leader had a magnetic personality, he negatively influenced his peers during regional staff calls and occasional meetings. This seed of negativity grew into a cancer of disengagement over the next several months—pulling the entire region into an intensive-care mode.

This situation underscored the importance of *preventive leadership* because once the disengagement process begins, it hogs our time and resources to reengage. Like cancer itself, there are no guarantees that your after-the-fact interventions will cure the disease. Proactively managing our health and our teams yields significant cost savings and productivity improvements. The landmark Gallup study estimated that the annual cost of disengaged employees was $300 billion— that's *billion* with a B![15]

A Gallup poll found only 26 percent of U.S. employees are fully engaged at any time. At the other end of the spectrum, 19 percent of employees are actively disengaged, meaning they intentionally act in ways that negatively impact their organizations. **The annual cost, nationwide, to employ this actively disengaged group exceeds $300 billion.**

—**Gallup Management Journal, 2001**

As the landmark Gallup survey, and others, has found, most employees are not engaged at work. Their bodies may show up every day, but their minds and hearts do not. If Passionate Performance ignites the light for your team to follow, disengaged team members can create a slippery slope toward the dark side.

Think of the last time you had to deal with restaurant servers who made it crystal clear that they had more important things to do than serve you. How did you get this impression? Possibly because it took forever for them to come to take your order—and even longer for them to bring your food. In the meantime, you were in need of a drink refill and, after looking around for a moment, discovered that your server had vanished into thin air. You finished your meal without anything to drink, and you waited for the check until you had to leave. Then you made your way to the hostess station and pleaded for your tab so you could get to your next appointment.

If you remember such a situation, you probably didn't have to think much farther back than last week.

That's where our challenge as leaders comes in. The minute, the very second, we see an engaged employee teetering on the brink of becoming disengaged, that's the time we need to act—not tomorrow or the next day, but right then.

So how do you know when employees are beginning to disengage? Here are some symptoms of disengagement:

- Increased turnover

- Missed deadlines

- Low morale

- High burnout rates

- Complacency

- Finger-pointing and name-calling

- Lack of accountability and responsibility

- Increased absenteeism

Since proactive leadership is the key to igniting Passionate Performance, our awareness of these and other symptoms is critical. Look for a relationship that is disintegrating. We might not see a particular team member around the office as much, his once enthusiastic spirit disappears, and the only time he'll talk is when you call a meeting. In fact, that once vibrant relationship diminishes to the point that neither of you is getting your needs met.

Another sign to watch for is when the employee becomes unhappy with her sales territory, her assigned projects, and/or her overall contributions. She doesn't feel like you're using her to her full potential. And, worse, she doesn't think you're doing enough to help her move to the next level.

Does any of this sound familiar? If you've answered yes, that's a sign that you have the cancer of disengagement growing in your team.

Some disengaged employees will choose to leave. That's unfortunate, but an even worse case scenario is if they stay on the job, just to put in time and be destructive.

That employee who quits? He'll no longer affect your organization. However, the actively disengaged employees who stay will have a toxic effect on everyone around them, and that includes your customers.

In fact, Gallup's survey also found that employees who are actively disengaged spread toxic mistrust and doubt in the organization's management and on the company's future.[16]

As a leader, this disengagement picture may seem pretty bleak, but don't take it too hard. Disengagement is simply the result of unfulfilled needs. These are basic human needs that leaders either forget to, choose not to, or simply don't know how to fulfill.

Disengagement is simply the result of unfulfilled needs.

100 Percent Commitment

Now that you've read about the challenge of igniting Passionate Performance in the last section, let's discuss the commitment that is required to make it a reality for your team.

As we have all learned through some of life's harder lessons—whether it's helping a friend through a tough time, coaching a little league team, or working on a critical project—**giving our best always gets the best results**.

The moment we totally commit ourselves and begin giving 100 percent, a certain momentum develops. People naturally gravitate to those who are committed and start working in the same direction. Total commitment results in a certain magical boldness—a boldness that has genius and power.

> **Total commitment results in a certain magical boldness—a boldness that has genius and power.**

Andrew Carnegie said, "The average person puts only 25 percent of his energy and ability into his work. The world takes off its hat to those who put in more than 50 percent of their capacity and stands on its head for those few and far between souls who devote 100 percent." **We compete against our own potential every day.**

I personally experienced the power of 100 percent commitment (and lack thereof!) when I wrestled with publishing a book for two years. I was consulting and writing leadership articles, and so I thought it might also be time to write a book. I went through all the motions, from working with agents to sending proposals to writers' conferences, but I never seemed to turn the corner from aspiring writer to a published author. There always seemed to be an obstacle, although I now realize it was a result of my less-than-full commitment to my goal.

One obstacle after another; two years and counting. Then one day I was at a client's office. My defining moment of commitment came when I saw a big box filled with practical handbooks sitting on my client's desk. I quickly flipped through one of them and jotted down the publisher's name as I said to myself, "I can do this!" My moment of commitment turned into action, and with the incredibly gracious support of the publisher, I had my first book in print six months later. My defining moment helped me envision possibilities that I could see only through fully committed eyes.

Our commitment to our teams can have the same transforming effect. Committed leadership inspires committed teams. During the most challenging time in history for the airline industry, as an example, Southwest Airlines' employees voluntarily forfeited $5 million in vacation time and $1 million in pay to help the company stay financially viable. Employees also took over the lawn and facility maintenance at corporate headquarters. These employees were simply reflecting a deep commitment-personal and professional— they felt from their leadership. When we lead with 100 percent commitment, this is the kind of commitment to engagement we can inspire in return.

Even with 100 percent commitment, however, leadership is not always a smooth flight. If we want to pilot our teams to full engagement, we have to understand that we can't just kick back in a comfy first-class seat. Now we have responsibility for not only ourselves but also for the safety and success of our teams. Our teams are depending on us to set a good course, keep them posted on our progress, and make smart decisions.

Jumping into the pilot's seat brings many more responsibilities than privileges. But those who are defined by their 100 percent commitment to Passionate Performance reap the rewards of flying high above the rest!

The Big Payoff

The hardest thing for your competitors to match is the most unique aspect of your organization—the hearts and minds of your employees.

Truett Cathy, founder and chairman of Chick-fil-A, the second-largest quick-service chicken restaurant chain in the country, built his business by engaging his employees. He calls it "the loyalty effect."

"As a chain, we believe that attracting great people helps create an unforgettable experience for our customers. It requires a lot of time and effort to make sure you have the right people working in the right jobs, but we believe this is time well spent. The bottom line is that our people, from our restaurant operators to the team members they hire, enjoy their work . . . and the more we can foster the feeling that we are a group of people working together, depending on each other, the more likely we are to be loyal to each other."[17]

He also puts principles and people ahead of profits. "I'd like to be remembered as one who kept my priorities in the right order. We live in a changing world, but we need to be reminded that the important things have not changed," he said.[18]

No doubt, Cathy understands the customer value chain and has intuitively built a culture of Passionate Performance. So, how can you identify Passionate Performance? Is it going on in your organization today?

The first clue is to look for the big payoff from Passionate Performance — discretionary effort.

Discretionary effort is people *willingly giving extra time and effort* **to help achieve the team's goals.** Some people call it "going the extra mile." You'll know your employees are giving discretionary effort when they:

- Choose to work late to complete a project.

- Ask how they can better serve another team member or department.

- Inquire about how their actions affect another function or the customer.

- Make a connection between their decisions and the company's financial results.

- Treat company resources like their own.

- Initiate improvements in work methods.

- Look beyond their own roles for improvement opportunities.

- Pursue self-development on their personal time.

Employees at Agilent Technologies serve as a good example of discretionary effort. Leaders throughout the organization work hard at engaging employees and helping them create strong emotional and intellectual attachment to their work.

Agilent spun off from Hewlett-Packard in 1999 as part of a corporate realignment. Its roots date back to 1939, when Bill Hewlett and Dave Packard started a company that shaped not only the Silicon Valley but the high-tech industry, as well. The founders were known not only for being ahead of the curve when it came to their products but also for their visionary approach to management, which became known as "the HP way." Their approach involved employee input, strong communication, recognition and reward, and intellectually challenging projects.

Agilent has continued the values that made Dave Packard and Bill Hewlett's company a success—dedication to innovation, trust, respect, teamwork, and uncompromising integrity. Agilent is also known for speed, focus, and accountability to meet customer needs and create a culture of performance that draws on the full range of people's skills and aspirations.[19]

During an economic downturn, the company was forced to eliminate more than 8,000 jobs. Because Agilent's leaders had developed an engaged workforce, they found many laid-off employees working until ten o'clock in the evening on their last day just to leave things in good order.

Now, that's Passionate Performance, and it can shine a light for your organization, even during dark times.

Passionate Performance takes many forms, including legendary customer service.

Let's revisit Nordstrom—the store where legendary service is the norm. The store, itself, was begun by John W. Nordstrom, an adventuresome teenager from Sweden who came to the United States in 1887, landing in Minnesota with a $5 bill in his pocket.

Working his way west, he paused briefly in Seattle before heading north to Alaska in search of gold. When he returned to Seattle two years later, he brought with him $13,000 from his find. There, he opened a shoe store in 1901 with a shoemaker named Carl Wallin. This was the start of what would become the retail legend of Nordstrom, Inc. In 1928, when the two partners retired, they passed the business to Nordstrom's two sons. In 1929 the Nordstrom boys expanded their downtown Seattle store, and the next year, in spite of the

Great Depression, their two stores made $250,000 in sales. Their next challenge came during World War II, when leather was rationed and each citizen could buy only three pairs of shoes per year. To fill the demand, the Nordstroms had to scrape to find enough available shoes to sell.

Once the war had ended, the Nordstrom brothers began building more stores, and by 1961 they operated 8 stores and 13 leased shoe departments. By 1980 Nordstrom was the third-largest specialty retailer in the country, operating 31 stores in California, Washington, Oregon, Utah, Montana, and Alaska.

Nordstrom increasingly came to be recognized as an efficient, full-service department store. Its leadership encouraged aggressive customer service, and this strategy plainly brought results.

In the 1980s the firm's customer service became legendary, as tales of heroic efforts by salespeople became legend: Clerks were known to pay shoppers' parking tickets, rush deliveries to offices, unquestioningly accept returns, lend cash to strapped customers, and send tailors to customers' homes.

An often-cited example of Nordstrom's legendary customer service occurred the day when a customer at the perfume counter couldn't find the bottle of perfume he wanted as a gift for his wife. Seeing the man's disappointment, the

Nordstrom employee asked if he could return in 20 minutes.

Twenty minutes later, the customer returned to find the perfume he requested, gift wrapped and ready to go. Because Nordstrom didn't happen to carry the brand of perfume the customer requested, the Nordstrom employee went to a competitor, purchased the bottle of perfume, and had it gift-wrapped and waiting for the customer when he returned.[20]

You too, can achieve these kinds of results when you fulfill the six work-related needs of your employees. You will create a powerful competitive advantage for your organization.

Even though the engagement strategies are simple, make no bones about it—they require lots of hard work. Yet, your hard work will be well worth the rewards of Passionate Performance. The journey can be compared to the process of planting an exotic Chinese bamboo seed. When this particular seed is planted and nurtured, it can take up to two years for a sprout to break through the earth. It requires the right watering, sunlight, care, and feeding so that it can build a strong root structure and foundation for growth, none of which is visible aboveground. However, once it breaks ground, this plant can grow over 100 feet in two weeks! The benefits of sticking to it are abundant with this bamboo seed—just as they are with employee engagement.

Yes, it does take time, but it does not cost a dime to engage your employees. So, let's take a look at what you can do right now to ignite Passionate Performance on your team.

The remainder of this book describes each need and offers practical strategies you can use to fulfill each one.

PART II

The Intellectual Side: Engaging the Mind

"Thought, not money, is the real business capital."
— Harvey S. Firestone, Founder,
Firestone Tire & Rubber Company

Engaging employees' minds tends to come naturally for many leaders. Why? Because the mind represents the intellectual aspect of an individual—the aspect based on reason, logic, and cause and effect. It requires the science of leadership, which is the focus of most leadership training and education. Engaging employees' hearts ignites their passion, and **engaging their minds builds employee performance**. Of course, bringing them both together yields Passionate Performance.

At one company, leaders look at each employee as an investment for the company. Taking the term intellectual capital to the next level, these leaders not only engage employees' minds, but they also nurture them and reinforce them with continuing training and opportunities to broaden their creative initiatives as well as their intellectual contributions. These leaders realize that employee performance can be elevated by engaging their employees' minds.

Engaging the Mind
the **Intellectual** Side
The **Science of Leadership**
Focuses on Cause and Effect
Based on Reason and Logic
The **BIG PAYOFF:**

IT BUILDS PERFORMANCE
OF YOUR TEAM!

Intellectual engagement involves the basics of leadership. However, as we all know, the basics are sometimes overlooked. Sometimes it is hard for us to keep our "eye on the ball." The world of professional sports illustrates this clearly. Most professional athletes practice 95 percent of the time and only perform 5 percent of the time. With all this opportunity to practice every little aspect of their sport, it is still not unusual for an all-star football receiver to take his eye off the ball just long enough to miss an otherwise easy touchdown pass. How many times have you seen an Olympic skier not stay in a tight tuck, catch a little air, and then eat snow well before the finish line? Or even a world-class golfer who forgets to shift his weight during a tee shot and shanks it into the water, never to see that ball again?

It's no shock that, as professional leaders, we sometimes don't perform the basics. The basics of the sport of leadership involve meeting our employees' three intellectual needs:

- Achievement

- Autonomy

- Mastery

When you fulfill these needs, you create a self-reinforcing cycle of improvement, growth, and high performance for your team. Your mind is a muscle. To grow and get stronger, it needs exercise, just as your biceps do. If it isn't exercised, challenged, and pushed to the next level, the mind will atrophy. Engaging the mind is a form of mental exercise; it strengthens your employees' ability to perform. If there's no regular exercise, no challenge, your employees' minds will become apathetic, constrained, and ultimately, disengaged.

Successful companies, like Southwest Airlines, have created cultures in which their greatest investment is in their employees who, in turn, are fully engaged in the company and deliver service that creates customers for life. Southwest's cofounder and former CEO Herb Kelleher once asked a friend who had just started a business, "So how's it going?" The friend groaned, "Herb, I'm spending 99.9 percent of my time on people." Kelleher responded, "Only 99.9 percent?"[21] Another expert "engager of the mind," Jack Welch, the former CEO of GE, said, "Any company trying to compete must figure out a way to engage the mind of every employee. Much of a company's value lies between the ears of its employees."[22]

Successful companies have created cultures in which their greatest investment is in their employees who, in turn, are fully engaged in the company and deliver service that creates customers for life.

So let's take a look at what you can do to become your own version of Herb Kelleher or Jack Welch.

"I always felt that my greatest asset was not my physical ability; it was my mental ability."
    –Bruce Jenner, Gold Medal Olympic Decathlete,

5

The Need for Achievement

"What you get by achieving your goals is not as important as what you become by achieving your goals."

–Zig Ziglar

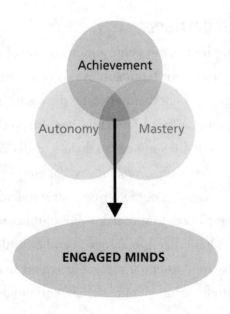

The need to achieve (diagrammed on page 51) is one of the more visible needs in our society today. This distinctly human need fuels performance in the worlds of sports, music, politics, media, and, certainly, business. We all have a need to achieve, and at one level or another, everyone wants to succeed at something.

An unfulfilled need for achievement leads to frustration, disappointment, and a decreased sense of self-worth. These are not feelings you want anyone on your team to experience. And you definitely don't want the reduced energy and productivity that accompanies these feelings.

Eliminate Barriers

Eliminating barriers to achievement is one of the quickest ways to help your team achieve. People naturally want to achieve results—for themselves, for the team, and for you. In fact, the human need for achievement is so strong that, for the most part, all you need to do as a leader is get out of the way! In other words, *make it easy for your employees to succeed*. This is not about lowering your standards. Making it easy for employees to succeed means eliminating barriers so that their basic need to achieve can be fulfilled. Some common barriers to employee achievement that you can control include: insufficient materials, equipment, or tools; lack of authority to accomplish goals; slow or unclear decision-making processes; undefined goals; poorly matched talents to demanding projects.

These barriers choke an employee's need for achievement rather than fulfill this important need. Here are a few actions engaging leaders take to eliminate barriers.

First, **be a resource provider**. Ensure that your employees have the necessary materials, information, introductions, access, equipment, and other resources to achieve their goals. It's important for you to have a good understanding of the work involved, from the key tasks to the critical milestones.

Second, **explain the game**. This action enables your team members to see the impact of their work. The challenge is that some leaders tend to fall short of explaining the game as clearly as their employees would like. In fact, leadership research supports this "explanation gap." A groundbreaking Harris poll of more than 11,000 households found that:

- Only 15 percent of workers could identify their organizations' most important goals.

- A majority of workers (51 percent) did not understand what they were supposed to do to help the organization achieve its goals.

- Less than half of available work time (49 percent) was spent on the organization's most important goals.[23]

In light of these findings, it's easy to see how an explanation gap can lead to an execution gap.

An explanation gap can lead to an execution gap.

In today's world of work, taking the time to provide a thorough explanation can easily take a backseat to more pressing leadership demands, firefighting, and troubleshooting. Try logging your firefighting tasks. How much of your time is spent on problems stemming from less-than-clear explanations of what, how, and why the game is played? **Explaining the game is a "pay me now or pay me later" leadership proposition.**

When you explain the game, you help employees see how they fit into the big picture. People will naturally feel more accountable for their achievement. Engaging leaders explain the game by consistently answering the *Fundamental Four* questions our teams are asking whether or not we actually hear them:

1. What are we trying to achieve?

2. How are we going to achieve it?

3. How can I contribute?

4. What's in it for me?

A closer look at these four questions illustrates that employees are really asking you to explain:

- Goals.

- Plans.

- Roles.

- Rewards (psychological, emotional, intellectual, and financial).

⩗⩘ PULSE POINT

1. On a scale of 1 (not well at all) to 10 (extremely well), how **clearly and consistently** am I answering the *Fundamental Four* questions for my team?____

2. Which of the four questions do I need to do a better job of answering in order to ignite achievement on my particular team?

_____

_____

3. What "baby step" can I take to better answer the question I selected above?_____

_____

_____

Your answers to the *fundamental four* questions create a bridge that connects today's possibilities with tomorrow's results!

The third way to eliminate barriers to achievement is to **match authority to responsibility**. Give employees the authority they need to achieve the results you expect. For example, at a large East Coast funeral home, a newly hired funeral director was on call when a community leader died and his new widow came to make arrangements. Because her husband had been in a highly visible role during his lifetime, the widow spared no detail as she planned his funeral, including selecting a seamless copper casket, the most expensive available.

When the widow left the funeral home, the young funeral director sent a bouquet of roses to the deceased's home, which was customary for every funeral service. The next afternoon, the director received a call from the widow, inquiring about when the funeral home would be sending a limo to transport her and family members to the funeral home for the visitation that night. "Because she had spent $50,000 on her husband's funeral," the young director explained, "I didn't hesitate. I told her a limo would be at her home promptly at 6:30 p.m., even though that wasn't the funeral home's usual offering."

When the director's leader discovered the decisions he had made, including sending a limo, free of charge, to transport the widow and her family, he smiled. "That's the accountability I wish I would see in every one of our employees. He did exactly the right thing to make this whole ordeal easier on the family."

This employee's responsibility for providing great service was aligned with his authority to make the necessary decisions. Imagine the scenario if he needed to make a few phone calls first to get approval for the limo. What would that customer interaction sound like, "Well, your business is very important to us (to himself, "Her business has helped us exceed our monthly revenue target"), but I need to see if I'm allowed to do that for you." It sounds ridiculous regardless of which end of the phone you are on! That's why engaging leaders ensure that their team members' authority matches their responsibility. There are few things more frustrating than being held responsible for a job and having your hands tied by your restricted level of authority.

Last, be decisive in order to eliminate barriers to achievement. Use the best available information and your intuition to provide definite and timely decisions for employees. **Analysis paralysis is the enemy of achievement**. Spending too much time deciding on or straddling an issue will soon sap every ounce of enthusiasm from your team. Engaging leaders use processes to drive decisions, not to delay them. They lead with confidence, knowing that every decision will not be perfect but that their decisiveness facilitates a sense of focus and clear direction. In short, it eliminates barriers.

Your job, as a leader, is to make decisions. **Business is not always a democracy.** Sometimes these decisions are based on input from your team or other departments. Other kinds of decisions may not permit polling others, so it becomes your job to make these decisions. Life and business reward action, so collect whatever data you can, and then make the best real-time decision you can. The 80/20 principle is a useful tool in being more decisive. This principle is pervasive in our world:

- 80 percent of traffic jams occur on 20 percent of roads.

- 80 percent of beer is consumed by 20 percent of drinkers.

- 20 percent of our clothes will be worn 80 percent of the time.

- 80 percent of our e-mails are from 20 percent of the senders (just check your inbox!).

Life and business reward action.

The 80/20 principle is also alive and well in business:

- 80 percent of profits come from 20 percent of customers/products/regions.

- 80 percent of problems are generated by 20 percent of the employees.

- 80 percent of sales are generated by 20 percent of sales-people.

- 20 percent of your stock takes up 80 percent of your warehouse space, and 80 percent of your stock comes from 20 percent of your suppliers.

Now take time out and look at the next paragraph. Go ahead, read it!

Cna yuo raed tihs? i cdnuolt blveiee taht I cluod aulaclty uesdnatnrd waht I was rdanieg. The phaonmneal pweor of the hmuan mnid, aoccdrnig to a rscheearch at Cmabrigde Uinervtisy, sguegsts that it dseno't mtaetr in waht oerdr the ltteres in a wrod are, the olny iproamtnt tihng is taht the frsit and lsat ltteer be in the rghit pclae. The rset can be a taotl mses and you can sitll raed it whotuit a pboerlm. Tihs is bcuseae the huamn mnid deos not raed ervey lteter by istlef, but the wrod as a wlohe. Azanmig huh? yaeh and I awlyas tghuhot slpeling was ipmorantt!

It's amazing how our minds are wired to make decisions, in this case to decipher words, with far less than complete information. We have this same capacity in our leadership roles. For many leaders, it is a defining moment the first time they use their intuition to "fill in the blanks" and make a real-time decision for their teams, just as we filled in the missing letters and rearranged the sequence of letters to read the above paragraph.

The 80/20 principle can help us make real-time decisions—smart and fast decisions. Imagine sorting all of the daily decisions you make into two piles—important and unimportant. Typically, only about one in five decisions will fall into the important pile. Don't hassle with or spend much time on the 80 percent of those unimportant decisions. In fact, try to delegate these. **Focus your efforts on the most critical 20 percent of the decisions**.

Go even further to apply the 80/20 principle to your important decisions. Gather 80 percent of the data in the first 20 percent of your time available, and then make the decision and act as if you were 100 percent certain! We should reapply our learning from 80/20 decision making. If our decision is not working, we should change our decision sooner than later. The real results of our decisions are a more powerful source of data than any hypothetical analysis we can do.

If our decision is not working, we should change our decision sooner than later.

On the other hand, if our decision is working, we should continue our efforts. Even if we do not yet fully understand why it is working, achievement is achievement. Of course, we should simultaneously try to identify the forces underlying our success.

Define Crystal Clear Goals

The second strategy for meeting the achievement need is to *define crystal clear goals*. Remember, as professional athletes in the sport of leadership, we must execute the basics consistently. One of the most basic, yet effective, way to meet the need for achievement is to define clear goals. This keeps your team accountable for measurable improvements and for hitting milestones along the way. To do this, engaging leaders work with their team members to write SMART goals:

- Specific
  - What will be accomplished?
  - With whom?
- Measurable
  - How will we know that the goal has been achieved?
  - How will we measure it? (Quality, quantity, cost, timeliness?)

- Attainable

  ○ Can the goal be accomplished?

  ○ Does the person responsible have control over the outcome?

- Relevant

  ○ How does this goal support our team's success?

  ○ What is the relative priority of this goal?

- Time-framed

  ○ When does this goal need to be completed?

  ○ When are the checkpoints?

The measurable and time-framed aspects of SMART goals tend to be the biggest barriers to sticking to them. Make sure you can fill in the blank, "I will know I have achieved my goal when _____." Once you know what result you are trying to achieve, you can determine if you are measuring the quality, quantity, cost, or timeliness of your performance. Be specific about when you want to achieve your goal—"next year" is not specific enough. Finally, state your goal positively, personally, and in the present tense. Although writing SMART goals can be tedious, those leaders who take the time to do so end up spending less time dealing with problems and more time boosting performance.

Comparing Ineffective Goals and Smart Goals

Ineffective Goal	SMART Goal
I will improve my efficiency.	I log all my tasks into my calendar and prioritize them based on what's most important for my team's success. I say no to my top three time wasters. I do not leave work until I finish all of my A priorities.
I will delegate better.	First thing Monday morning, I identify the key tasks for our team that week and match them with team members' skills. I spend 10 minutes with each team member to ensure that they know what is required. I provide the resources team members need to complete the tasks I have delegated to them.
I will build a better culture on my team this year.	I have regular meetings with all team members individually to better understand what I can do to help them succeed. At least once a month, I identify a team accomplishment worth celebrating.

〰〰 **PULSE POINT**

Write a SMART goal for an important project you are currently working on.

_____

_____

_____

_____

_____

Now, check to ensure that it meets the SMART criteria, that it is:

- Specific.

- Measurable.

- Achievable.

- Relevant.

- Time-framed.

Remember, blurry goals lead to blurry places. Crystal clear goals make your team shine!

Once you have agreed to clear goals, you have to stay focused on them. To illustrate the importance of staying focused, consider two sources of energy: the sun and the laser. The sun is a powerful source of energy that showers the earth with billions of kilowatts of energy every hour. Yet, with minimal protection—like a hat and some sunscreen—you can bask in the sunlight for hours with few negative effects. The laser, on the other hand, uses a weak source of energy and *focuses* it in a cohesive stream of light that produces intense heat and power. With a laser, you can drill a hole in a diamond or even cure certain types of cancer. That's the power of focus!

It works the same for your employees. Crystal clear goals require less energy to yield greater results because your employees' efforts are focused, laserlike. Clear goals make it easier for employees to achieve because they can better prioritize their time and energy to focus on things that are important to your team's success.

If clearly defined goals are so powerful and support employees' need to achieve, why do so many leaders struggle with diffused employee efforts? The primary reason is today's change-intensive, information-loaded business world. This type of environment creates so many distractions that it's hard for employees (and leaders) to stay focused on their

---

Crystal clear goals require less energy to yield greater results because your employees' efforts are focused, laserlike.

goals. These distractions steal time and energy and can quickly undermine your employees' efforts to achieve.

I recently read this saying on a poster: "When winds of change blow hard enough, even the most trivial of objects can become deadly projectiles." Invest the time to define and continually reinforce employees' goals to help them see clearly through the winds of change—and achieve!

Fulfilling the Need

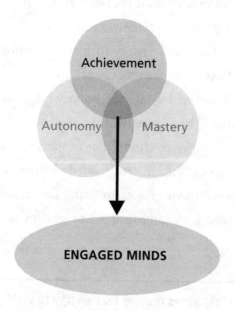

Key strategies to fulfill your employees' need for *achievement* include:

- **Eliminate barriers to achievement.**

  - Ensure that your team has the resources to achieve the results you want.

  - Explain the game by answering the *fundamental four* questions:

    - What are we trying to achieve? (Goals)

    - How are we going to achieve it? (Plans)

    - How can I contribute? (Roles)

    - What's in it for me? (Rewards)

  - Match authority and responsibility levels.

  - Be decisive. Apply the 80/20 principle to:

    - Focus on the most critical 20 percent of decisions.

    - Gather 80 percent of the data quickly and then make the decision as if you were 100 percent certain.

- **Define crystal clear goals.**

  ○ Write SMART goals with my team:

    –Specific

    –Measurable

    –Achievable

    –Relevant

    –Time-framed

One action I can take to more effectively meet this need is:_____

_____

_____

_____

_____

6

The Need for Autonomy

"If you put fences around people, you get sheep."
–WILLIAM McKNIGHT, FORMER CEO, 3M

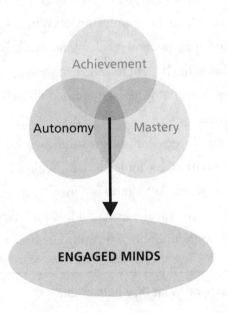

While achievement focuses on the *outcome* of your employees' work, autonomy focuses on the *process* of getting work done. Engaging leaders give their teams the freedom, or autonomy, to determine the best way to perform their jobs. These leaders realize that employees have a basic need to "own" or control their work.

Involve Your Team

The first strategy to fulfill this need is to *involve your employees* in defining and improving their work processes. Clearly defined processes are critical to any efficient operation. Even in the most routine jobs, you can still get input from employees about ways to make improvements. When you give team members the appropriate level of autonomy, you engage their minds. What is the benefit to you? People support what they help create. And that leads to increased discretionary effort from employees.

Giving employees control over their work is not always intuitive or comfortable for leaders. It requires that they have trust in their team. Autonomy is generally more important than doing it "the way the boss said to do it." What's the risk of not providing autonomy? Employees basically become

---

People support what they help create.

robots; they give you their hands and feet, but not their minds and hearts. However, engaging leaders realize there is more than one way to effectively solve a problem. An employee's approach might be different from the leader's, but the benefits of establishing ownership that come from employees creating the solutions far outweigh any loss of control leaders might feel.

The simplest tool to use to involve your team members in improving their work is also the most underused tool. It is the single, most powerful leadership tool we have... listening. Understanding the two types of organizational knowledge helps underscore the importance of listening. The two types of organizational knowledge are **dashboard knowledge** and **under-the-hood knowledge**.

Dashboard knowledge is typically used by leaders. Just as your car's dashboard tells you the speed, fuel level, and engine temperature, your organizational dashboard tells you if "sales are up 5 percent," "productivity is down," or "project deliverables are on schedule."

Under-the-hood knowledge is specific to a given job, time, place, and set of circumstances. While dashboard knowledge is important for understanding general relationships and charting broad direction, it is not helpful in identifying specific actions, improvements, and adjustments to help your team run more smoothly. Under-the-hood knowledge determines why your team's engine is running hot, why it veers to the right, and why it is not responding to the brake pedal as well as it should. **This is the kind of knowledge you can get only from people who are currently working "under the hood."**

For example, Atlas Container Corporation used under-the-hood knowledge to make a critical vendor decision. Executives asked shop-floor employees to choose between competing suppliers of a $1 million machine they needed for their operation. The employees selected an American-made model, so the top executives accepted their recommendation, even though they favored a different model.

The Atlas leaders knew that under-the-hood knowledge just wouldn't show up on their dashboard. They had to ask questions to get it. They also understood the key to asking questions is to listen, really listen to the answers. **Don't ask if you won't listen.** Asking without listening only builds cynicism and dampens the spark of engagement. Remember what Mark Twain said: "If we were supposed to talk more than we listen, we would have two mouths and one ear." **Engaging leaders listen at least 50 percent of the time.**

~~~~ **PULSE POINT**

Think of a typical day on your job (if there is such a thing). What percentage of the total time you interact with others do you spend listening compared with talking? _____%

Consider asking more clarifying questions to fully understand all perspectives, assumptions, and opinions so you can make the best decision with your team.

Clarifying questions are:

Open-ended. They force deeper thinking and ownership responses from employees. Closed-ended questions, which require only a yes or no response, put the accountability right back on you to ask a follow-up question (an autonomy crusher).

Specific. An open-ended, general question is usually not very useful. Ask for specific details and data to help your team create the best solution to the issue at hand.

Not embedded with solutions. Be careful to avoid a subtle or inferred solution or preference in your questions. Your goal is to collect information; then solutions will quickly follow.

Ask more clarifying questions, and you will find yourself listening more and building greater autonomy!

If you're not listening to your employees, you will gradually suffer from "blind spots"—weaknesses that are apparent to others but not to you. A classic episode of *Seinfeld* provides a great illustration of blind spots. It featured Elaine while she was the acting president of her company. She couldn't figure out why her entire staff was suddenly shying away from her. She quickly blamed her friend George for her seeming downfall at the office. This all started to happen after a company party where Elaine, thinking she was a good dancer, did not hesitate to show off a few of her moves. Unfortunately, this was a *huge* blind spot for Elaine. It was painfully clear to everyone else that Elaine was a horrible dancer as she flailed and contorted her way across the floor!

As a viewer, you could feel the tingle of embarrassment for her and the dread if you should ever find yourself in such a situation. Fortunately for Elaine, she had an incredibly blunt friend in Kramer who, in no uncertain terms, revealed her blind spot saying, "You stink!"

Learn from Elaine. Listen to your employees, particularly your "Kramers."

Engaging leaders prevent blind spots by making concerted efforts to stay in tune with the realities of their employees-listening for the truth.

This is particularly important because **the higher you are in an organization, the more filtered the information you receive**. It's a natural and predictable phenomenon, but it's also a precarious position for any leader. No leader wants to be "Elaine on the dance floor." Therefore, the higher your leadership position, the more listening you need to do. Ask your employees what they think, **listen to their answers**, and you will take an important step toward fulfilling the need for autonomy.

Leaders at Toyota do a great job of involving employees and fulfilling their need for autonomy. Toyota employees are required to submit two suggestions per month that they can implement themselves or with a teammate—in other words, something the employee can control. As a result, Toyota receives about 1.5 million employee suggestions for improvement each year. More impressively, 80 percent of these actually get implemented and save the company $300 million annually!

Virtually all of these ideas are implemented at the employee level. Problems and improvements are identified, solved, and measured by each team—the experts in their jobs. It's not the company mandating these improvements; rather, accountability and results are driven at the frontline team level, where the rubber meets the road.

Even though many of Toyota's employees perform repetitive jobs, they are fully involved and engaged in improving their work output and their work lives. This approach sends a strong message that employees have control over their work processes.

It's no surprise that Toyota has now inserted itself into America's "big three" automakers. This unprecedented market share gain is powered by a healthily met need for autonomy. What kind of impact would this approach to autonomy have in your organization?

Inspired by Toyota's success, the chairman and CEO of Dana Corporation asked his 80,000 employees to submit two creative ideas per month and to implement 80 percent of them. For more than 10 years Dana's employees implemented about 2 million ideas per year, saving the company over $2 billion.

And this idea keeps on working. Subaru averaged 108 ideas per employee which resulted in savings of $39 million. This equated to savings of $5,000 per employee. **These amazing results required no executive approval or committees.** That's autonomy at work!

Set Broad Yet Clear Boundaries

The second key strategy to fulfilling the need for autonomy is to *set broad yet clear boundaries*. Jeff Immelt is chief executive officer at General Electric. One of his leadership tips is: Manage by setting boundaries, with freedom in the middle (in other words, give your employees autonomy). He says,

"The boundaries are commitment, passion, trust, and teamwork. Within those boundaries, there's plenty of freedom."

Boundaries are also often referred to as rules of engagement. They help define how your team will interact. They are like the "we card" signs you see in every convenience store. Those signs were created to help the store workers.

In the past, convenience store workers had to ask each customer wanting to buy alcohol or tobacco for identification to ensure that he or she was of legal age. This became awkward for the store workers. They had to visually assess who might be close to legal age (not a position I would want to be in). As a result, they had to risk the legal implications if they did not ask for identification from someone who was not of age. They also had to deal with the wrath of those who were offended by being asked for identification.

Today, with the help of "we card" signs, workers only have to point to the sign. No fuss, no risks, nothing personal. It's a rule of engagement that is understood by all parties.

Defining the rules of engagement for your team can yield similar benefits. They create accepted ways of acting and interacting so that your team does not have to think about or debate what is appropriate in each situation.

Think back to your school days. Each teacher, usually on the first day of the year, explained the classroom rules of engagement: Raise your hand if you have a question, request a hall pass to use the restroom, place your homework on your desk each morning, respect others' property, etc. These rules helped both the teacher and students focus on the most important things in the classroom-learning.

Defining the rules of engagement can help your team focus on what is most important—performance. Rules of engagement might address how to:

- Make decisions.

- Share information.

- Consider ideas for improvement.

- Coordinate hand-offs between departments.

- Review work.

- Challenge prevailing thought.

- Prioritize.

- Resolve conflict.

Look to your team and company values for hints of appropriate rules of engagement. They will help you define the playing field within which employees can use their skills and creativity to get work done.

They do not have to be wordy, but they must fit your team and be embraced by team members. Here are some examples:

- All reports must be reviewed by at least one other team member before leaving our department.

- If an issue is not resolved after five e-mails, you must meet (by phone or in person) to resolve the issue.

- Customer-related tasks always have a higher priority than internal tasks.

- No team or committee meetings last more than one hour.

- Every project is debriefed for lessons learned within one week of project completion.

- Speak your mind during meetings, not after.

- All problems must be presented with a solution (my personal favorite!).

Engaging leaders keep their rules of engagement visible and apply them to decisions they make—even small decisions. They also rely on their entire team to ensure that each member (including themselves!) is performing within the rules of engagement. In other words, they lead and work by these rules.

⟨♒⟩ PULSE POINT

1. What are some rules of engagement your team uses?_____

_____

_____

2. Would your team be able to recite these? _____
Don't leave it to chance:

- Discuss your rules of engagement with your team.

- Ensure that each team member publicly agrees with them (or even signs a copy).

- Publish them. Post them in every office and in meeting rooms.

- Vigilantly uphold them, and your team will soon follow.

Do these things, and your team will find comfort in these behavioral boundaries and feel autonomy to perform within them.

When team members work within boundaries and are provided with autonomy, they will take personal pride in their work and:

- Identify improvements you likely would not—because they're closer to the work and to the customer.

- Use their discretionary time and effort to measure and monitor their own processes (like business owners, they will demonstrate similar efforts as owners of their processes).

- Increase quality and quantity of output (they will feel a sense of accountability to themselves and their team).

- See a clear connection between their work and the goals of the team (true process owners ask, "How does this process affect our team and our customers?").

Involve employees in improving their work processes and set clear boundaries; then you will engage their minds and be on your way to Passionate Performance!

Fulfilling the Need

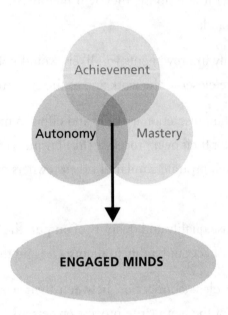

Key strategies to fulfill your employees' need for autonomy are:

1. **Involve employees in improving their work processes.**

- Ask your team for improvement ideas:
    - ○ Make it easy for them to implement ideas.
    - ○ Focus on quantity of ideas versus quality.

- Listen at least 50 percent of the time in order to:

    ○ Tap into your team's under-the-hood knowledge.

    ○ Prevent blind spots.

2. **Set broad yet clear boundaries.**

- Agree to rules of engagement for how your team will:

    ○ Make decisions.

    ○ Share information.

    ○ Consider ideas for improvement.

    ○ Coordinate hand-offs between departments.

    ○ Review work.

    ○ Challenge prevailing thought.

    ○ Prioritize.

    ○ Resolve conflict.

- Within your broad yet clear boundaries for performance, let your team determine the best methods to achieve their goals.

One action I can take to more effectively meet this need is:_____

7

The Need for Mastery

"In teaching others, we teach ourselves."

—Proverb

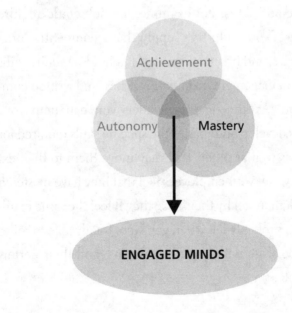

One of the strongest intellectual drives of the human species is to be able to do something well—to master something. We're born with this need. Consider, for example, the toddler who is learning to walk. Despite hundreds of trips, tumbles, bumps, and bruises, a baby's need to master the skill of walking remains strong until he or she can do it effortlessly. Remember yourself at age five or six. Just as everyone around you had learned to ride a bicycle without training wheels, you endured countless crashes until—at last—you could ride down the sidewalk, alone and unfettered by training wheels.

In the workplace, mastery is about being competent in a given position. A single role can require different types of knowledge and skills. For example, one job could require knowledge of your industry's supply chain, competitive pricing, strategies, and financial metrics. It may also require skills in project management, negotiation, sales, and written communication. As an engaging leader, you can help your employees develop and master the specific skills required for their jobs as well as others that may move them to the next level. And when your employees feel that they have mastered the skills demanded by their jobs, they'll feel the same exhilaration you probably felt when you were finally able to roller skate or ice skate without falling down—and their performances will soar.

Ensure the "Highest and Best Use" of Employees

Finding a good fit between an employee's natural abilities and interests and the requirements of the job is crucial to meeting the mastery need. Just as land developers look for the "highest and best use" of a parcel of land to maximize the return on their investment, engaging leaders view themselves as people developers. They look for the highest and best use of their employees by taking time, at the front end of a project, to match people to positions. This matching process is the single-best predictor of how well the mastery need will, eventually, be met. If you don't match the employee and the role correctly, you are double-stacking the odds against your team. First, it's unlikely that the employee will master the role which will result in frustration—a precursor to disengagement. Second, without a thoughtful match, it's more likely that your project will be unsuccessful.

Think of it this way. Most types of sports equipment—a golf club, a tennis racket, a baseball bat—have a certain spot that, if the ball hits it, will give the player the optimal result.

Engaging leaders view themselves as people developers.

Hitting this sweet spot yields a long drive down the fairway, a swift crosscourt return, or a home run swing. Every piece of sports equipment has a sweet spot of some type. If you have experienced it, you know that when you hit the sweet spot, you barely feel it. The ball goes exactly where you want it to go—even farther and faster that you'd imagined. Doesn't get any better than that! As leaders, we have a huge opportunity to help our employees find their sweet spots, too. This ensures the "highest and best use" of their talents. Wouldn't we just love having every single team member working in his or her sweet spot and being perfectly fitted to the job? We would always be in "the zone," and work would feel like play.

Did you know that the average person possesses between 500 and 700 different skills and abilities? Mastery is achieved when we find that skill or ability that's the equivalent of our sweet spot.

Let's not forget about ourselves in this matching process. Gaining insights into our own sweet spot as leaders helps us better determine how to design roles and deploy the talent on our team. For example, if my sweet spot is conceptually designing complex deals, I had better be sure I have a strong analyst on my team. If my sweet spot is analyzing lots of details and numbers, I want some conceptual, big-picture thinkers on my team.

〰️ PULSE POINT

Want to know an easy way to find your sweet spot? Look at the intersection of these two questions:

1. What am I absolutely passionate about?

_____

_____

_____

2. Which tasks are very easy and natural for me to perform?

_____

_____

_____

Most of us vividly remember when we found our professional sweet spot. Others told us that we made it look easy, that we really excelled, and that we looked like we were having a ball. Think of the last time when others made these comments to you. What were you doing?_____

_____

_____

Like finding any sweet spot, it's worth hitting these questions around for a while and practicing our answers before we can serve up a winner.

Ralph V. Gilles understands the process of finding the sweet spot. He dropped out of college and was spending most of his time — by his own admission — slacking in his parents' basement, eating granola, watching *Dukes of Hazard* reruns, and lamenting the sorry state of automobiles being made in America.

Growing up, Gilles was typical of most boys who played with Hot Wheels and Formula 1 model cars. But as a teenager, he also was extremely talented in sketching vehicles. In fact, his aunt wrote a letter to then Chrysler Chairman Lee Iacocca suggesting that he should hire her 14-year-old nephew.

A Chrysler executive responded, recommending three design schools. Soon afterward, however, the letter was lost and forgotten. Meanwhile, the car-crazy Gilles completed high school and enrolled in college to study engineering, but he dropped out quickly. His reason: "I was in a funk, and was really not sure I wanted to be an engineer."

As he continued his granola–*Dukes of Hazard* routine down in the basement, Ralph's older brother, Max, recalled the letter from Chrysler. He remembered that one of the recommended schools was Detroit's College for Creative Studies. Upset to see Ralph wasting his time and talent, Max pushed his brother to apply to the local school although the application deadline was only a week away and would require 10 sketches.

At that point, the whole family became involved, making Ralph coffee so he could complete his sketches, cheering him on, and helping wherever they could. By the end of the week, Ralph was covered in pencil lead, but the sketches were complete, so his mother sent the packet to the school by overnight delivery.

Today, Ralph V. Gilles is recognized as the innovator of the Chrysler 300 sedan and the Dodge Magnum Wagon I in addition to being responsible for the 2002 Jeep Liberty, 2003 Dodge Viper SRT-10, and several concept cars. Dubbed as the Chrysler Group's newest darling at the time, Gilles has earned numerous national and international accolades. He has since been promoted to design director for Chrysler.

If we consistently misidentify sweet spots, we will find our team stuck in a funk, like Gilles. If we correctly match employees' sweet spots to the job requirements, we will all be living the sweet life!

Today's fast-paced, efficiency-minded organizations make it especially challenging for leaders to always ensure a good fit. It's common to find employees picking up the slack for positions that have been eliminated. If personnel reductions aren't executed carefully, the remaining employees can find themselves *under*employed — consumed by "leftover" tasks that drain their time but don't tap their minds. These situations start a cycle of "lowest and worst use" of talent, resulting in a downward spiral of self-doubt, anxiety, and frustration.

If you've ever experienced this, you know it feels more like a sour patch than a sweet spot. More like misery than mastery.

To prevent this cycle and the resulting decline in team performance, we can plan the work for our teams to optimize sweet spots by:

- Combining tasks that require similar skill levels so that we can more easily match an employee's sweet spot with a position's requirements.

- Automating repetitive tasks.

- Streamlining inefficient processes and eliminating redundant tasks that rob us of getting the highest and best use of our talent.

- Outsourcing tasks that require a high level of people power but have little impact on our organizations. Stay within our own sweet spots and let other vendors use their sweet spot to serve us.

Seize Teachable Moments

The second strategy for meeting the mastery need is *learning*. **When you invest in a mind, you engage it.** Mastery is not built in chunks. It's a gradual process of layering to create a rich, multilayered learning environment for your employees. This happens when you use a variety of learning sources—special projects, cross-function assignments, and training colleagues. The best test of learning is to be able to teach what you've learned to someone else. Layer by layer, each experience will lead to mastery. There are few places where you can better spend your leadership resources than in building your team's mastery. Engaging leaders achieve results *through* others. Your employees' mastery will ultimately get *you* the results you need to move the team to the next level.

Do you know your employees' best and most important source of learning? It's you! **An engaging leader is a coach**, so share your experiences. There are lessons to be found in every step of your career with every project your team undertakes. Look for teachable moments for your employees through postproject reviews, customer meetings, conflicts and their resolution, changes in priorities, miscommunications, and mistakes—yes, even mistakes! The truth is that good judgment comes from experience, and a lot of our experiences come from bad judgment. Seize all these opportunities to coach your employees toward mastery.

At one time, Andrew Carnegie was the wealthiest man in the United States. He came to the United States from his native Scotland when he was a small boy, did a variety of odd

> **The best test of learning is to be able to teach what you've learned to someone else.**

jobs, and eventually ended up as the largest steel manufacturer in the United States. At one point, he had 43 millionaires working for him. In those days, a millionaire was a rare person.

A reporter asked Carnegie how he had hired 43 millionaires. Carnegie responded that those men had not been millionaires when they started working for him but had become millionaires as a result of working for him. The reporter's next question was, "How did you develop these men to become so valuable to you that you have paid them this much money?" Carnegie replied that men are developed the same way gold is mined. When gold is mined, several tons of dirt must be moved to get an ounce of gold, but one doesn't go into the mine looking for dirt—one goes in looking for the gold.

Some leaders find themselves sitting on a mountain of gold, and yet they feel poor because they don't know how to mine the gold from their teams. **Engaging leaders coach good employees to become better people**. They help them build better lives for themselves and others. They build their employees from the inside out—inspiring mastery at work and in life.

In the crunch of daily demands, we sometimes forget a **fundamental law of leadership: If our employees are successful, we are successful**. Engaging leaders are crystal clear on this law and focus on nurturing success and inspiring mastery.

When my son was 11 years old, he earned his junior black belt in karate. Of course, I was very proud of him, because he had come a very long way since his first lesson. I remember that lesson well. He was seven years old, and one of the first things "the master" taught him was a simple exercise called a kata. This kata ended with the beginning student saying emphatically, "V for victory and bow for humility," as he crisscrossed arms over his head with fists clinched for the V and then bowed forward for humility.

That night, he came home from his lesson and quickly ran to me, bursting with pride to show me what he had learned. Seeing his enthusiasm, I dropped what I was doing and became an intent audience of one. As he finished the kata, he performed the closing "V for victory, bow for humility!"

But then, to my surprise, he started yelling insults at me: "Man, I took you down! How about that buddy!" and so on. More than a bit shocked and confused, I asked, "Hey pal, what was *that* all about?" He responded in a very matter of fact manner, "Dad, that's the bow for humility."

Well, this pointed out how such a little thing can make a big difference—he thought it was a bow for *humiliation*, not humility.

My son heard his instructor's performance expectation but made his own (incredibly misdirected) interpretation based on his own perceptions. As leaders, if we depend on others' perceptions to meet our expectations, we will be disappointed every time. As a result, we need to communicate more clearly, specifically, and frequently than we typically think we need to. Fear not. We clarified that definition of humility with my son before he earned his black belt!

> **If we depend on others' perceptions to meet our expectations, we will be disappointed every time.**

Another coaching challenge is that we remember only **20 percent of what we hear.** Let's take a closer look to understand why this percentage is so low. Let's say that I am hurried and swing by an employee's cube and say, "Ryan, please make sure you use the new format on the month-end sales report. Thanks." Even if Ryan is a pretty sharp guy, what do you think the chances are he will hear my request accurately, remember it, recall it accurately when it's relevant, interpret my instructions as I intended, and then perform the task satisfactorily?

When we look at it this way, 20 percent sounds pretty good, doesn't it?

Effective coaching minimizes recoaching on the same topic. If we are coaching employees on the same thing repeatedly, before we get frustrated with them, we need to ask ourselves, "Am I inspiring learning, or am I just checking this off my list?" "Am I handing out a memo with instructions, or am I asking the employee to perform a task while I give him real-time feedback?"

The coaching hierarchy below helps us understand why sometimes we get caught in a recoaching cycle. We must push our coaching effort to the top of the coaching hierarchy to improve retention because we generally remember. For example, if someone on my team is struggling to comply with a defined sales process and I give him a memo outlining that process, he is likely to remember only 10 percent of the information because he is reading it. To move up the coaching hierarchy, I could spend a few more minutes and have him tell me his understanding of the process, clarifying it for him if necessary. After that, I could have him demonstrate it with a real customer while I observe and provide helpful feedback afterward. Now, this employee is likely to retain 90 percent of the information because he said and did something.

90 percent of what we both say and do (simulating the real thing, doing the real thing).

70 percent of what we say (participating in a discussion, giving a talk).

50 percent of what we hear and see (watching a movie, looking at an exhibit, watching a demonstration).

30 percent of what we see (looking at pictures).

20 percent of what we hear (instructions).

10 percent of what we read (memos, books—that's why I have chapter summary pages to help increase your retention!).

〜〜 PULSE POINT

First, write down a recent coaching interaction you have had and the approach you used to communicate with the other party. _____

_____

_____

_____

_____

Second, identify where your coaching approach falls on the coaching hierarchy. Think of how **your employee, not you, experienced the coaching.** For example, if I told an employee what she should have said to calm an upset customer, she is only at the 20 percent level of retention (she heard my instructions).

Based on your coaching method, what percentage of your message would you expect your employee to remember? _____%

Now, consider how you might adjust your coaching method in the future to push higher on the coaching hierarchy. Taking this new approach next time will reduce your chances of having to recoach on this same issue.

In the example with my son, he heard his performance expectation (20 percent chance of remembering) but made his own interpretations from there. Well, this happens on our teams every day, and it's up to us to ensure effective coaching of our teams—minimize recoaching and maximize mastery.

Coaching is another pay-me-now or pay-me-later leadership proposition. Take a shortcut, and you will be saying the same thing to the same employee next week—no fun for either of you.

Fulfilling the Need

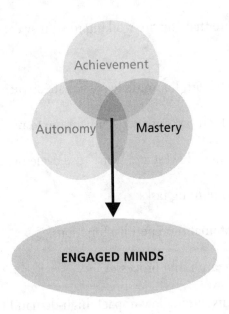

Engaging leaders invest their time in coaching right the first time. Coach them now, or coach them later. The choice is ours.

Challenge your employees in every way, every day. *They* will master their jobs. *You* will engage their minds and elevate your team's performance.

Key strategies to fulfill your employees' need for mastery include:

1. **Fit person to position for "highest and best use."**

- Design jobs so that each employee is working in his or her sweet spot.

- Ensure that you are working in your sweet spot by asking:

  ○ What am I absolutely passionate about?

  ○ Which tasks are very easy for me to perform?

- Prevent a "lowest and worst" use cycle by:

  ○ Combining tasks.

  ○ Automating repetitive functions.

  ○ Streamlining processes.

  ○ Outsourcing low-impact, high-demand tasks.

2. **Seize teachable moments to coach employees.**

   - Teach others and thereby teach yourself.

   - Mine for the "gold" in your employees.

   - Coach employees to be better people, not just better employees.

   - Use coaching methods toward the top of the coaching hierarchy to prevent recoaching.

   One action I can take to more effectively meet this need is:_____

   _____

   _____

   _____

   _____

   _____

PART III

The Emotional Side:
Engaging the Heart

It's not the size of the man, but the size of his heart that matters.

—EVANDER HOLYFIELD, THREE-TIME WORLD
HEAVYWEIGHT BOXING CHAMPION

The heart represents the emotional side of people that is based on connections. Engaging the heart ignites passion. This side requires the art of leadership that focuses on relationships.

In today's high-velocity world, it's easy to get caught up in current management fads and really only pay them lip service. Isn't it easier to say you're doing something, even if you're not, especially if it's a new trend that many people or organizations are embracing? In the 1990s, every organization was singing the praises of diversity. However, only a small percentage of these companies were actually diversifying the ranks of their employees. Fortunately, today it's a different story. Before diversity, we saw companies jump on the "empowerment" and "reengineering" bandwagons. Based on generational values and workforce supply, the "engagement" bandwagon is here to stay. In order to hop on this bandwagon, we must engage our team members' minds *and* hearts. That sounds pretty soft to many of us.

The softer side of leadership is more challenging. It's the art of leadership that relates to dealing with emotions, relationships, and connections. Traditional leadership development programs don't often emphasize the softer skills necessary to engage employees' hearts, and many organizations don't reinforce these skills with their leaders.

Engaging the Heart—the Emotional Side.

The **Art of Leadership**

**Focuses on Connections to Purpose,
        to People, and to Contributions
Based on Relationships**

The **BIG PAYOFF:**

IT IGNITES PASSION IN YOUR TEAM!

> **We live in a world driven by emotional decisions.**

As a result, many leaders tend to be less comfortable with the softer side of leadership because they simply never learned how or what to do. Although we might like to think otherwise, the truth is that we live in a world driven by emotional decisions. Remember, 70 percent of customers' buying decisions are based on positive human interactions— usually a one-on-one between customer and salesperson or the company representative. Likewise, employees are primarily driven by emotional and personal considerations. When people go to work, they don't leave their hearts at home. We may live in a high-tech world, but **leadership is still a high-touch job**.

How often do you hear people speak with envy about companies with "real heart"? Companies like The Container Store, Harley-Davidson, Enterprise Rent-A-Car, and Chick-fil-A, to name a few? Outsiders are constantly looking for their "secret" to success. The secret lies in the hearts of their employees. These companies created connected teams and as a result built dominant businesses.

To ignite your team's heart, you must fulfill three basic emotional needs:

1. Purpose
2. Intimacy
3. Appreciation

When you fulfill these needs, you create self-reinforcing connections:

- Between your team's work and the organization's mission (purpose).

- Among each other (intimacy).

- Between your employees and you (appreciation).

These connections establish strong, intangible relationships that yield amazing tangible results. Engage employees' hearts, and watch their passion grow!

Let's take a closer look at each of these three emotional needs and how we can fulfill them.

> **We are employed by organizations, but we work for people.**

8

The Need for Purpose

It's not enough to be busy. The question is, what are we busy about?
— HENRY DAVID THOREAU, POET AND NATURALIST

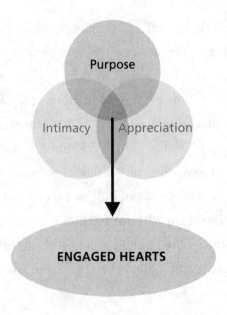

All of us are in search of a clear and driving purpose for our lives. As human beings, every one of us wants to contribute to something bigger than ourselves—that burning desire that drives our work efforts.

Think about your personal history to validate this need. When you were in elementary school, for example, didn't you get a special sense of satisfaction from participating in a school play, collecting cans for needy families at Thanksgiving, or working on that huge mural in art class?

In high school or college, wasn't there special gratification from being part of a team or organization? Didn't you have a sense of fulfillment building a float for the homecoming parade or working on a volunteer project—something that was bigger than you?

Today's workplace offers a great opportunity for people to connect with a purpose. The reality is simple: People care less about working for a company than they care about working for a compelling purpose. **Meaning precedes motivation**. Our purpose answers the most fundamental question, "Why do we do what we do?" Without a compelling purpose, without something bigger than themselves to focus on, your team members just put in their time. **A team without a purpose is a team without passion**.

Picture this: Three people were crushing rocks side by side on a construction job. When they were asked, "What is your job?" the first person answered, "My job is to do what I am told for eight hours a day so I can get a check." The second person replied, "My job is to crush rocks." The third person said, "My job is to build a cathedral." Which of these three people do you think would be the happiest and the most productive? Which would go the extra mile? No doubt the third person, who understood that his job was far greater than just crushing rocks. He understood that he was contributing to a purpose greater than his own efforts.

When people work hard for something they believe in (as if they were owners of your business), a high degree of passion develops. **This passion cultivates a mental toughness that enables employees to see opportunities in situations that might be seen only as obstacles by others.** Creating a sense of purpose for employees and developing that passion elicits discretionary effort and a willingness to sacrifice for the greater cause.

Create a Compelling Purpose

Take a close look at what your employees are doing, day in and day out. You might find that their hearts are much bigger than their jobs. Get team members fired up and inspired about a compelling purpose, and their hearts will follow. **A**

purpose is your team's bridge to a brighter tomorrow—and you have to build it!

Before you spring into action, it's important to realize that a project goal is *not* a purpose. Neither is a financial target or a strategic plan. Most (nonsales) employees will not get emotionally charged up about a 10 percent net profit, a 20 percent return on investment, or a 30 percent increase in market share. Here's the difference: A compelling purpose is a reason to be excited about getting up and going to work every day—like Google employees, who want to be part of the effort to organize the world's information and make it universally accessible and useful, usually within a fraction of a second.[24] Remember, we are talking about the emotional side of engagement.

A purpose can come in a variety of forms. Perhaps it is to help others, to make the world a better place, or to innovate the best products in the industry. At Disney, for example, the compelling purpose of each Disney employee is to "make dreams come true." Coca-Cola employees continue to work diligently to achieve its purpose—to put a Coke within reach of every person on Earth. Not surprisingly, what do you think Pepsi's purpose is? To beat Coke!

Google gives prospective employees a list of 10 reasons to work for the organization. Number one is, "Lend a helping hand." The second reason begins, "Life is beautiful. Being a part of something that matters and working on products in which you can believe is remarkably fulfilling."[25]

Your organization's purpose may not be immediately apparent. For instance, I worked with a company that distributes building products to homebuilders. Their purpose did not seem very exciting to their leadership team or to the employees. Yet a deeper look revealed that this company was a key link in the distribution chain of getting raw building products to sites where homes were being built for first-time home buyers. In essence, this company realized that they helped make the American dream (of home ownership) a reality. This new, deeper sense of purpose was really worth working toward.

Your team may have a purpose of its own. It might simply be to support the purpose of the organization. If that's the case, help your employees make a strong emotional connection between their individual roles and the organization's purpose. Engaging leaders don't wait for their organizations to communicate a purpose. Instead, these leaders take the initiative to engage the hearts of employees so that they will be able to develop a passion for their work. No matter how large or small your team, define a compelling purpose.

The "why?" question is the most important motivational question a leader can answer. Sometimes it's the hardest question because it requires a deep look at your business. For example, at one customer call center, the purpose is to brighten the day of every caller. An IT department's purpose is to improve personal productivity. At a certain purchasing department, the purpose is to ensure that all products are made with the best raw materials available. I remember talking to a client who worked as a dishwasher at a local hospital during college. She relayed how her boss did a great job of connecting her routine job to a bigger, emotionally compelling purpose. She said, "I never thought of my job as a dishwasher because from the first day on the job my boss made it clear that our purpose was to help maintain a clean, safe environment so our patients could go home as soon as possible." Wouldn't you be more committed to washing dishes if that were your cause? This leader really got the connection between the need for purpose and emotional engagement long before any labels were assigned to them.

⩘ PULSE POINT

First, write a rough draft of your team's purpose:

1. Think about why your team exists.
2. Be bold! Most people's hearts are bigger than their purpose.
3. Take a step back and look at the big picture.

4. Answer the questions, "What difference are we making?" and, "Aside from making a profit, why do we do what we do?"

After you have *drafted* your team's purpose, answer the following questions:

1. Does my team feel that it is emotionally compelling?
2. Does it show how we make the world a better place? Improve life or conditions of:

   - Colleagues?

   - Company?

   - Customers?

   - Community?

Last, consider input from your team and revise your draft. It might take a while to really get to the true purpose of your team, so take your time. If you try to just zip it out, you might fall short of igniting the passion you want from a purpose-driven team.

We must also keep our compelling purpose real and relevant because **people can commit** *only to what they understand*. In Fact, Warren Buffett, arguably one of the best investors of our time, invests only in businesses that he can understand in just a few minutes. In other words, he will commit (his money) only to what he can understand.

For nine consecutive years, Wegman's Food Stores, a 71-store grocery chain that began as a fruit and vegetable market in Rochester, New York, has been named one of the top places to work in the United States by *Fortune* magazine. In 2005, it was named the number one place to work. In 2007, it was number three. So, why are these supermarkets in demand? Perhaps their slogan says it all—"Making a difference in our community." Or maybe it's because leadership at Wegman's believe that, "Good people, working toward a common goal, can accomplish anything they set out to do . . . and in this spirit, we set our goal to be the very best at serving the needs of our customers. We also believe that we can achieve our goal only if we fulfill the needs of our own people."[26]

To engage your team the way Wegman's does, ask team members how their jobs relate to your team's purpose. Some questions you might pose include:

- How does our purpose make you feel? (If you hear responses like *proud, important, connected, helpful, or like a winner,* then you're on the right track.)

- Does our purpose make you look at your job differently?

- Do our roles, procedures, resources, skills, and priorities support our ability to achieve our purpose?

- What can you change or do differently to better support our purpose?

- What can I change or do differently to better support our purpose?

Let your team members help you define their own connection to the team's purpose and what they can do to perform more purposefully.

Happiness comes from following one's passion. Success comes from work that you are passionate about.

—ANONYMOUS

Stay Focused on Your Purpose

Once employees see a clear connection between their roles and their purpose, the second strategy to meet the need for purpose is **to help them stay focused on that purpose.** In today's multitasking world, it is easy to become preoccupied with activity and lose sight of meaningful productivity. If we do not lead our employees to focus on the purpose, they can get caught up in activities ("I'm really busy") instead of their productivity ("I'm working toward our purpose"). If we do not help our teams stay focused on our purpose, it is easy to drift off course. Then we have to pay the price with our precious resources—time, money, and energy—to get back on course. Even if we get back on track, there are untold lost opportunities that we missed by spending our precious resources to get refocused.

I like the story Charlie Jones told to help illustrate the importance of staying focused on what matters most—your purpose.

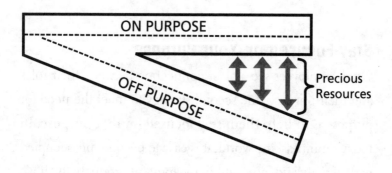

Leading on Purpose

Charlie Jones is a sportscaster who has covered several Olympic games in his long career. At the 1996 games in Atlanta, he was assigned to announce the rowing, canoeing, and kayaking events—a situation that left him less than thrilled, since these events were broadcast at 7 a.m., and the venue was an hour's drive from Atlanta.

What Jones discovered, however, was that these events ended up being among the most memorable of his career because he gained a chance to understand the mental workings of the Olympic athletes who participated in them.

Preparing for the broadcast, Jones interviewed the rowers and asked them about conditions such as rain, strong winds, or breaking an oar. Each time the response was the same: "That's outside my boat."

After hearing the same answer again and again, Jones realized that these Olympic athletes had remarkable focus. In their attempt to win an Olympic medal, he wrote: "They were interested only in what they could control . . . and that was what was going on inside their boat."

Everything else was beyond their control and not worth the expense of mental energy that would distract them from their ultimate goal.

Jones wrote that this insight made the event "by far the best Olympics of my life," and it changed his thinking in other parts of his life as well.

We all remember the moments when we had to redirect employees' efforts back "inside the boat" to keep our team focused. I remember having to jump overboard a few times to rescue employees who had drifted way outside our boat!

We can stay inside our boat by focusing our precious resources on our purpose.

Our time, energy, and money are precious resources; if we spend them in one area, we cannot spend them in another area. They are finite. As a result, **saying yes to one thing always means saying no to something else**. Communicating this message deep into our team enables employees to say No to non-value-added tasks and to stay focused inside the boat—on our purpose.

One important way to demonstrate a team's focus is to say no to activities that do not support its purpose.

Saying no helped Walgreens to outperform the stock market average 15 times between 1975 and 2000. At one point, Walgreens owned more than 500 restaurants. It decided that its future was in convenience drugstores and that it would be out of the restaurant business in five years. Walgreens redefined the boat. It courageously stuck to its commitment, which required saying no many times to ensure a redirection of resources to its new future.

Saying no also applies to the day-to-day decisions we make as leaders. For example, if we spend two hours in a meeting that does not help our team achieve its vision, we pay an opportunity cost by spending time on non-value-added tasks. If we find ourselves saying, "That was a waste of time," or, "Why was I attending that meeting?"—these are signs that we need to say no.

Meetings are an important way to conduct business. When I call a meeting, I think about the salaries of each attendee and the potential time he or she could be working on other important goals instead of being at the meeting. Since leaders decide how to use their employees' time, they must ensure a good return for their time investment. Of course, meetings can be both necessary and useful, but they can also diffuse our focus if we do not know when to say no.

PULSE POINT

To help focus your **precious resources**—time and energy—on your team's purpose, before you accept an invitation to another meeting, ask the meeting sponsor these four questions:

1. What is the meeting's objective?
2. What role do you want me to play in the meeting?
3. What materials do I need to review in advance to ensure that the meeting is an effective use of time for all involved?

4. Based on the agenda, what portion of the meeting do I need to attend so we can avoid underutilizing my time?

These questions are even more powerful when you give your team permission to ask them before meetings they are invited to.

Your teams will feel the same relief that you feel when you find ways to stay on-purpose without going to unnecessary meetings. Ask these questions, and you will find more time to work on your purpose—guaranteed!

Your employees' time and energy are precious resources. If they are spent on one nonproductive task, there will be nothing to use on a productive activity. Communicating this message deep into your team enables employees to say no to non-value-added tasks and to stay focused on executing your plan. Saying yes to one thing always means saying no to something else. If you try to be everything to everyone, you'll be nothing to everybody.

When you give employees a purpose—and you fill their hearts with passion—they won't just be engaged. They'll be in overdrive!

Fulfilling the Need

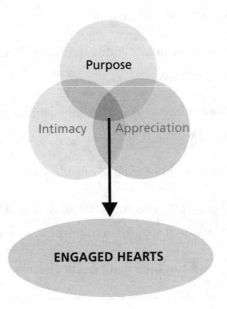

Here are some key strategies to fulfill your employees' needs for *Purpose*:

1. Create a compelling purpose.

    -   Ask yourself and your team, "Why do we ultimately do what we do?"

    -   Keep the purpose real and relevant—we can commit only to what we understand.

- Help employees see the connection between your team's purpose and their job.

2. Stay focused on activities that directly support your team's purpose.

- Use your purpose to make daily decisions about what to do and what not to do.

- Don't worry about what's "outside your boat."

- Focus your precious resources of time and energy. Say yes to tasks that support your purpose and no to others.

One action I can take to more effectively meet this need is:_____

_____

_____

_____

The Need for Intimacy

People don't care how much you know until they know how much you care.

—UNKNOWN

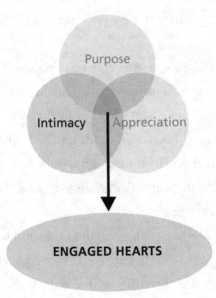

Intimacy makes people feel connected. It's the basic human need to belong.

Back in your childhood, you may have belonged to a club that had a secret handshake. Just knowing that handshake made you feel that you were a part of the group. That handshake was the "intimacy" factor that made you feel connected. There was something special that only members could do or know.

In your work life, a need for intimacy means feeling a part of a team and being connected to those around us. When this need goes unmet, you feel alone and disconnected. Without intimacy, you morph into a set of hands punching a clock. If you don't feel connected to others, you come to work each day, but you leave your heart at home. You disengage.

Next fall, when you see geese heading south for the winter, flying along in V formation, you might consider what science has discovered about why they fly that way. As each bird flaps its wings, it creates an uplift for the bird immediately following. By flying in V formation, the whole flock adds at least 71 percent greater flying range than it would have if each bird flew alone.

People who share a common direction and sense of community can get where they are going more quickly and easily because they are traveling on the thrust of one another. When a goose falls out of formation, it suddenly feels the drag and resistance of trying to go it alone and quickly gets back into formation to take advantage of the lifting power of the bird in front of it.

When the head goose gets tired, it rotates back in the formation, and another goose flies point. It is sensible to take turns doing demanding jobs, whether with people or with geese flying south.

Geese honk from behind to encourage those up front to keep up their speed. We all need encouragement along life's journey.

Finally, when a goose gets sick or is wounded by gunshot and falls out of formation, two other geese fall out with that goose and follow it down to lend help and protection. They stay with the fallen goose until it is able to fly or until it dies; and only then do they launch out on their own, or with another formation to catch up with their group.

Nothing we achieve in this world is achieved alone. It is always achieved with others helping us along the way. If we use the approach of the goose, we will stand by each other. Geese are defined by how they stay connected to one another. Engaging leaders and high-performing teams are defined the same way. Both strategies to fulfill the need for intimacy are based on building relationships and close connections, and your team should be the focal point for developing these connections.

From reading this excerpt from Google Corporation's Web site, it is clear that the company's leaders understand the importance of meeting the need for intimacy:

> Google is not a conventional company, and we don't intend to become one. True, we share attributes with the world's most successful organizations—a focus on innovation and smart business practices comes to mind—but even as we continue to grow, we're committed to retaining a small-company feel. At Google, we know that every employee has something important to say, and that every employee is integral to our success.[27]

Maintain a Sense of Smallness

Our coworkers and immediate supervisor significantly influence how we relate to and feel about our organization. This is because the smallest team is where the closest relationships are developed. Close connections are more likely to be sustained on smaller teams. Small teams allow for more intimacy between employees and customers (internal or external) and among team members. As organizations grow, more layers are naturally created between the customer and the top executive. This expanding hierarchy inhibits a team's speed, responsiveness, and real-time understanding of customer needs. This results in diminished ability to deliver

> **The smallest team is where the closest relationships are developed.**

good, fast service to customers. Additionally, as teams expand, employees may not only find it harder to keep their fingers on the pulse of the customer but they may also find it harder to stay connected with other team members.

In the early years of BMC Software, for example, teams were small—from administration to product development. Everybody knew everyone, and it was simple to keep the corporate goal in sight. As the organization grew from slightly over 200 to more than 6,000 workers, this "intimacy" disappeared as teams got bigger and bigger. Unfortunately those employees who needed smaller groups dropped by the wayside. Those who didn't need those close connections continued their careers there. Why was the intimacy lost at BMC, even as it became more successful and stock prices climbed?

As organizations grow, most of the time (but not always) they become more bureaucratic. The organization, as it grows larger, needs larger staff functions to handle administrative functions. Some bureaucracy, of course, is essential, and administrative procedures can often help improve organizational efficiency. That said, when it comes to engaging

> **If you cannot feed a team with two pizzas, then the team is too big.**

the heart, even large, worldwide organizations depend on local leaders to build connections and foster intimacy.

On smaller teams, people generally feel more connected, more informed, and more part of the big picture. Close connections are more likely to be sustained on smaller teams, and these connections extend from the team members to their customers. That's why Microsoft keeps its development teams at around 12 members—to foster close connections with their customers. That's also why Amazon invokes the "two pizza rule." If you cannot feed a team with two pizzas, then the team is too big.

Small teams also facilitate deeper relationships within the teams. People want to feel that they have "family" at work. The more employees feel those familylike emotional attachments to their coworkers and the organization, the more emotionally engaged they will be. They will help each other and take care of each other at work—and often beyond work. Some other advantages of small teams include: establishes a higher sense of mutual accountability and commitment (minimized diffusion of responsibility); keeps team members closer to customers and their needs; improves team agility; facilitates knowledge of all team functions (good bench strength) so that each team member fully understands and internalizes the team's purpose.

This theory is borne out at St. Luke's Episcopal Hospital in Houston, where a member of the nursing staff was becoming more and more ill because of a failing kidney. After finding no organ donors in her family, the woman went to part-time status, trying to maintain an income, in spite of her failing health. That's when a coworker, another RN, stepped up and offered to be tested as a donor. When it was determined that she was a perfect match, the potential donor did not hesitate. "We are family here," she said. "I couldn't sit by and do nothing. I didn't want to watch her die." The transplant proved successful, the once-ailing nurse is back to full-time status, and the bond between her and the donor, which was strong before, is even stronger now.[28]

PULSE POINT

1. What are you doing to create a sense of smallness on your team?_____

   _____

2. What can you do to help your team create close, familylike connections?_____

   _____

   _____

When employees form close connections, they become passionate about their work. Gallup's research found that those who responded that they work with a close friend are also more likely to be engaged in their jobs.[29] They are those employees who go above and beyond what is expected—for each other and for the team.

Not long ago, I was walking near the receiving dock at the back of a store location for a national retailer. I watched as an entry-level clerk in his early 20s abruptly stopped an empty truck before it left the loading dock. Quickly grabbing a broom, he hopped into the back of the truck, gave it a good once-over with the broom, and then motioned for the driver to go ahead.

After the truck pulled away, I walked past him and jokingly said, "Nice jump back there."

He replied, "Well, I'm done with my shift, but I wanted to make sure the truck was cleaned up. It saves Jeff time back at the warehouse when he picks up another load. Jeff's on my service team, and he's had a pretty hectic schedule this week. I just wanted to help him out so he could get home to his family earlier. No big deal."

Now, that's the power of a connected team!

Create Rituals and Celebrations

The second strategy for meeting the intimacy needs of your team members is to create rituals and celebrations. Engaging leaders do what other leaders may consider to be corny. These leaders make it a priority to **establish rituals that connect employees to each other and to the customer.**

Time out! Read this:

> The country's royalty lined up, side by side, dressed in their full regalia and crowns that identified their region. They stepped forward to pay homage to the leather treasure that is symbolic of their common bond. The king then handed the leather treasure to one of his compatriots, who proceeded to swiftly deliver it to his fellow citizens from his region who were seated quite some distance from him. However, the other royal family did not seem to be cooperating in the delivery. When the leather treasure was finally delivered, some of the citizens expressed their appreciation with applause and cheers while others shook their heads in disappointment.

What ritual have I just described?
A football team scoring a touchdown!

〰️ PULSE POINT

Our rituals create the fabric of our culture, and they are critical for building connections within our teams. Once we establish deeply ingrained team rituals, we view them as "the way we do things around here" just as we don't think twice about how we cheer for a home team touchdown, but it can look rather strange when we take an objective view. For an eye-opening view of your team's rituals, pretend you are a Martian visiting your team. Walk around the office or plant and take note of only the observable behaviors. Then, see what those behaviors tell you about your team's rituals.

- Do people "check in" with each other before getting to work in the morning?
- What is the reaction if a big new deal is closed—lots of hoopla or business as usual?
- What role does food play during the workday?
- How do meetings get started and wrap up?
- How are special occasions handled?
- What role do social and community activities play on your team?

We can create rituals around hiring, recognition, production, innovation, heroes, quality, promotions, family, customer service, community service, learning, and so on. Whatever form the ritual takes, it creates connections. Rituals connect our team members to each other, to us, and to our purpose. Select rituals that fit your leadership style and the chemistry of your team. **Effective rituals feel natural for you and must be performed with 100 percent reliability.** If on "Last Friday Birthdays," you celebrate all team members' birthdays in that month, but you forgot to do it twice last year, then it's not a ritual. Rituals are predictable, expected, and reveled in by teams. They can be as simple as:

- Celebrating employees birthdays.

- Having a different team member share a "success tip" to kick off each staff meeting.

- Posting photos of new team members and new customers.

- Volunteering at a local charity event.

- Having a unique, fun way of introducing new employees.

- Having last-Friday brown-bag lunches (you pick the topic for discussion).

- Ringing a bell when a big sale is made.

- Sharing a high and low moment from the past week during each staff meeting.

Yum! Brands is the world's largest restaurant company that includes Taco Bell, KFC, Pizza Hut, Long John Silver's, and

> **Rituals connect our team members to each other, to us, and to our purpose.**

A&W. To start each staff meeting, team members all do the YUM! cheer, and it's an honor to be asked to lead it. Everyone participates, every time, with everything they have! Trust me. I've been a guest during a meeting and have done the cheer myself. Sound corny? Not at all. It is an energizing and fun way to connect a team and start a meeting—a powerful ritual!

Markeeta Graban, associate director of the department of psychiatry at the University of Michigan Health System, reports, "It's really true that anything can be a significant form of recognition. Over three years ago, I drew a star on a piece of scrap paper, colored it, and gave it to someone for helping me out that day. They, in turn, gave it to someone, who gave it to someone else. It took on special significance with each use. Now we have it on a magnetic backing and pass it on to someone who has helped or is having a rough day. People love it!"

During stressful times at Maritz Performance Improvement Co. in Missouri, leaders use the "Thanks a Bunch" award. Someone brings in a bunch of flowers to give a hardworking employee, who keeps one flower and a thank-you card but passes on the remaining bunch to another performer who, in turn, repeats the process. At the end of the day, they collect all the cards and draw for prizes.

Team rituals do not have to be focused inward. Many organizations, large and small, build rituals around how they help the community, whether it's tutoring at local schools, helping with fund-raising races or walks, visiting hospitals, or working on beautification projects. For example, Kimberly-Clark Corp. spent $2 million and had thousands of employees help build playgrounds in 30 needy communities.

Even America's low-cost retailer has a highly ritualized culture. For those of you who are unfamiliar with the Wal-Mart cheer, it goes something like this: A leader yells, "Give me a W," and the Wal-Mart associates (employees) yell back, W. Each letter is, in turn, yelled and echoed back, culminating in the rousing cheer, "WAL-MART!" But the most delightful aspect is the Wal-Mart wiggle. Employees get to shake their booties to represent the hyphen in Wal-Mart, an experience that creates a brotherhood/sisterhood bond among associates who are then overcome with the urge to sell and serve Wal-Mart customers.

Who doesn't feel special when their leader takes the entire department to lunch the day before a holiday? Who doesn't bond during a retreat away from the office? Who cannot forget the fancy-dress dinner party that celebrated the achievement of a corporate goal? The purpose of every one of these events is to foster intimacy, belonging, and fun—and I can assure you that the employees who take part in these activities do not think of them as corny.

Engaging employees' hearts is a personal matter. Maintaining small teams and creating rituals help fulfill your team's need for intimacy. If employees cannot build close relationships with their team members, it's unlikely that they will be successful in building the necessary relationships with your customers. Connect your team with something fun, simple, and meaningful. Start with just one ritual, stick to it, and don't compromise it. A good team achieves its goals, but connected team members help each other succeed!

Fulfilling the Need

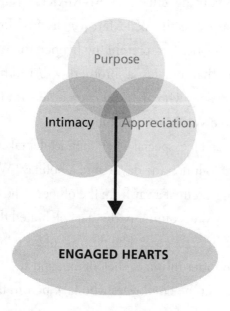

Here are some key strategies to fulfill your employees' need for *intimacy*.

1. Maintain a sense of smallness.

    *   Create more, smaller teams as you grow rather than fewer larger teams.

    *   Apply the *two pizza rule* to manage team size.

2. Create rituals and celebrations.

    *   Identify your existing rituals by taking an objective look at the behaviors of your team.

    *   Ensure that your team rituals feel natural to you and your team.

    *   Keep it simple.

    *   Focus on only one or two new rituals to ensure 100 percent reliability in performing them.

    One action I can take to more effectively meet this need is:_____

    _____

    _____

The Need for Appreciation

People will forget what you said. People will even forget what you did. But people will never forget how you made them feel.

—UNKNOWN

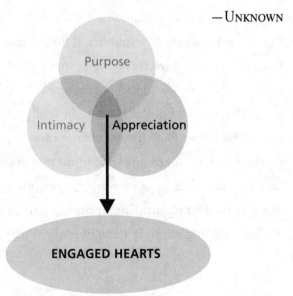

William James, the father of modern psychology, saw the need to be appreciated as a fundamental human need. This assertion is still valid in today's world of work. People who work hard for an organization want to feel appreciated for their work, whether the appreciation is demonstrated publicly or privately. The leader who believes that people need no recognition and that they should be content simply to have their jobs will never see Passionate Performance from his or her employees.

Although most leaders recognize the need for employee appreciation, this tends to be a blind spot for many. Why? Because leaders generally believe that they are much more appreciative of their employees than their employees think they are. Here's my explanation for this blind spot based on my own experience. The number of times I heard myself say things like, "Boy, Grace is doing a super job. I will need to let her know," or, "As soon as I get around to it, I need to do something special for Alex because he really pulled us out of a jam!" far outweighed the number of times I actually acted on these best of intentions. The blind spot appears because we judge ourselves by our intentions, but others judge us by our actions. **Demonstrating appreciation is not a matter of time and intention. It's a matter of priority and action.**

Appreciate Contributions

Appreciation for employee effort, commitment, enthusiasm, and passion is considered to be the best and the most cost-effective way of retaining employees and boosting their discretionary effort and your bottom line. Appreciation is also remembered much longer than is a bonus or a plaque. And appreciation makes the employee feel connected and valued.[30] The bottom line: **We do more for those who appreciate us**.

Although cash bonuses and gift cards are one way to acknowledge contributions, they rarely are powerful enough to engage your employees' hearts. On the other hand, *non-cash* appreciation—like the parking space in front of the building is not only powerful but is also longer-lasting. Why? Because it's personal, it's visible, it builds relationships, and it builds connections with employees. As a result, it engages the heart of the recipient.

Research by the former chairman of Gallup, Donald Clifton, revealed that work groups with at least a three-to-one ratio of positive to negative interactions were significantly more productive than those having less than a three-to-one ratio.[31] In other words, more productive teams had at least three positive interactions for every one negative interaction. By the way, the same study showed that the bar was set even higher for more successful marriages—the key ratio was five to one.

> 〰️ **PULSE POINT**
>
> What's the ratio for your team? Is it 1:1, 3:1, 5:1, or 10:1?
>
> Track your team's ratio for a week to gauge how well you are appreciating your employees' contributions. Look for moments to acknowledge your team's efforts. Reinforce those behaviors that you want to see more frequently. Catch team members doing something right. Then acknowledge it, and do so often!

When people become aware of something—in this case, opportunities to recognize performance—they tend to see more of that thing. I call this the *yellow car phenomenon.*

When was the last time you saw a yellow car? You might see a yellow car once a day or so (except taxicabs for those who live in big cities). Now, for the next week check out how many yellow cars you see.

Since I have alerted you to yellow cars, you will probably observe many more of them than you had previously noticed. Is it because so many more yellow cars just hit the streets? Of course not. You just focused your mind on yellow cars, and like a magnet, you see more of them. I first experienced the yellow car phenomenon when my wife was pregnant with our first child. Being the happy-go-lucky yuppie, I rarely noticed an expectant mother, but now that my wife was expecting, I saw expectant mothers all around. I thought to myself, "Boy, there must be something in the water here in Dallas." Well, of course there wasn't. I had just heightened my awareness of the state of pregnancy. It was the power of my personal focus. Recognition works the same way. When we focus on people doing a good job, we see more people doing a good job. In fact, they're all around us!

Demonstrating our appreciation for employees and their efforts can put them on the fast track to full engagement. There should be plenty of opportunities since a Harris poll found that 65 percent of workers reported receiving no recognition for good work in the previous year![32] Don't worry about recognizing your teams too much. To date, **there are no documented studies of employees ever feeling *over*-appreciated**!

Great recognition can even come from a moment of spontaneity. A Hewlett-Packard engineer once burst into his manager's office to announce that he'd just solved a problem the group had been struggling with for weeks. His manager, obviously grateful but unprepared, quickly groped around in his desk for an item to acknowledge the accomplishment. The only thing he could find was his lunch bag, so he rummaged around inside it and pulled out—a banana! He handed the employee a banana from his lunch with the words, "Well done. Congratulations!" written on it. Initially, the employee was puzzled, but in time the "Golden Banana Award" became one of the most prestigious honors bestowed on an inventive employee in that division. Now, that's going bananas with recognition!

FedEx is well known for using a planned way to spontaneously recognize employees. They call it the "Bravo Zulu" award. Bravo Zulu is a Navy term meaning "well done." FedEx managers reward employees for outstanding efforts and achievement on the spot. Rewards include "quick cash" bonuses, theater tickets, dinner gift certificates, or even a simple note with a sticker of the Bravo Zulu flag on it.

Appreciation is certainly not a one-size-fits-all gift. It should be customized—in essence we need to **personalize employee recognition**. For example, being recognized at an all-employee meeting might trigger more perspiration than inspiration for an introverted employee. Instead, use the information you learn about your employees to present an appropriate gift, token, or sincere expression of appreciation. Invariably, the gift will be less important than the obvious time and thought that went into it.

The great news is that leaders have lots of control over this type of appreciation. No budget limitations here, because there are literally thousands of ways to appreciate your employees' contributions at little or no cost. It should be memorable, sincere, personal, and meaningful to the specific employee being recognized. When it comes to employee recognition, the goal is to outthink your competition, not outspend it. Here are just a few ideas to get your gears churning:

- Say thank you — an all-too-obvious but seriously under-used form of appreciation.

- Allow employees to present their work to your boss. This is a great way to engage employees and open communication between employees and upper-level management. It also shows your boss what kind of leader you are.

- Offer team leaders their choice of projects to work on. Simply assigning projects takes away their input and their empowerment. It also allows employees to buy in to a project, and when they buy in, they put their hearts into that project.

- Put a sincere acknowledgment for contributions made into your company or department newsletter. While this takes only a few minutes of your time, it creates a long-term "trophy value" for employees. Plus they can send it to family members, showing their progress in their careers.

- Tell an employee's story of accomplishment at a staff meeting. Stories are perceived to be more interesting, meaningful, thoughtful, and memorable than simply droning out facts.

- Take a team member to lunch to show your appreciation when she or he goes the extra mile, comes in early, stays late, or puts in monumental effort to meet deadlines and accomplish project goals.

Appreciate the Person behind the Employee

The engaging leader also knows that *appreciating the person* is just as important as appreciating contributions. As Wal-Mart's Sam Walton said, "Outstanding leaders go out of their way to boost the self-esteem of their people."

After interviewing 25,000 leaders, Ferdinand Fournies found that the most effective leaders had one thing in common—they expressed a sincere interest in their employees.[33] "Sincere" is the operative word here. Our motivation matters! If we appreciate employees in hopes of getting something in return, they will see right through us.

When I was a leader in a corporate setting, I remember thinking that I was really good at appreciating my team. One of my employees would always come through if an emergency came up on the weekend. I really appreciated him,

> **The only statistically significant factor differentiating the very best leaders from mediocre ones is caring.**

and I could always bank on one particular employee to take on the big projects and make winners out of them. I really valued her. However, in retrospect, I realize that I really only appreciated their contributions and not necessarily who they were as people. It took a whole new level of maturity for me to understand that appreciating my employees as people was a win-win approach to management. Employees feel appreciated and as a result are willing to give more discretionary effort—to go above and beyond.

People don't care how much you know until they know how much you care. This particularly holds true for employees and their leaders.

～ PULSE POINT

How do you demonstrate to your team members that you are sincerely interested in them?_____

_____

_____

_____

_____

Consider integrating check-in points into your normal routine. For example, never take a direct route to the restroom (unless necessary, or course!), meetings, or lunch. Build in an extra few minutes to zigzag your way to your destination. While you're on the way, stop off to check in with a team member or two.

Avoid turning these check-ins into project updates. Ask about employees' weekends, kids' activities, spouse's new job, their garden, upcoming vacation, and so on.

Look for common ground—something you are both interested in—to ensure that your interactions are sincere and heartfelt.

We need to show our teams we care by staying plugged in. Today's technology offers many options—Blackberries, pagers, cell phone text messages, instant messaging, voice mail, e-mail. Be cautious of overuse of these communication options. Remember, we work in a high-tech world, but leadership is still a high-touch job. With all these technology options, it's easy to find ourselves too busy for face-to-face interaction, but face to face is one of the best ways to charge up our teams.

Learn something new each day about one of your employees. Ask them about their families, hobbies, leisure activities, and the like. You will begin to understand and appreciate them more fully. Then weave this information into your interactions with them. They will return your appreciation with passion for your leadership.

Appreciate your employees, and you will engage their hearts!

Fulfilling the Need

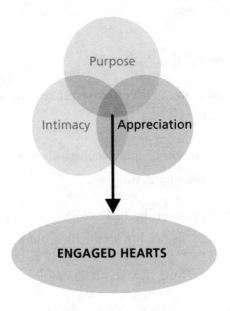

Key strategies to fulfill your employees' need for *appreciation*:

1. **Find opportunities to appreciate employee's contributions.**

- Ensure that you have at least a three-to-one ratio of positive to negative interactions on your team.

- Look for and reinforce those behaviors you want to see more of (remember the yellow car!).

- Make your employee recognition:
  - Personal
  - Memorable
  - Sincere
  - Meaningful

2. **Demonstrate a sincere interest in your employees as people.**

- Help the *person* become successful, and the *employee* will become successful.

- Don't rely entirely on technology to stay in touch with your team—leadership is still a high-touch job.

- Learn something new about an employee each day.

One action I can take to more effectively meet this need is:_____

_____

PART IV

Igniting the Fire

To get Passionate Performance, you must give it.

After leaving the helm of General Electric in 2001, Jack Welch and his wife, Suzy, penned a book titled, *Ideas the Welch Way: How Healthy Is Your Business?* A primary focus of this book is employee engagement.

As the former GE CEO has said, "Employee engagement comes first. It goes without saying that no company, small or large, can win over the long run without energized employees who believe in the mission and understand how to achieve it."

Without a doubt, engaged minds build your employees' performance, and engaged hearts build their passion—these two go hand-in-hand. You, the leader, ignite Passionate Performance only when all three intellectual and all three emotional needs are fulfilled and you connect employee hearts and minds. Table IV-1 summarizes the strategies that should be followed to fulfill the six needs we have discussed.

Needs	Strategies
Intellectual	
Achievement	• Eliminate barriers to achievement. • Define crystal clear goals.
Autonomy	• Involve employees in improving their work processes. • Set broad yet clear boundaries.
Mastery	• Fit person to position for "highest and best use." • Seize teachable moments to coach employees.
Emotional	
Purpose	• Connect roles to a compelling purpose. • Stay focused on activities that support your purpose.
Intimacy	• Maintain small teams. • Create and reinforce team rituals.
Appreciation	• Find opportunities to appreciate employees' contributions. • Demonstrate a sincere interest in your employees as people. Learn what makes them tick.

11

Leading the Way with Courage and Humility

With courage you will dare to take risks, have the strength to be compassionate and the wisdom to be humble. Courage is the foundation of integrity.

—KESHAVAN NAIR

Taking a stand, for anything, requires courage. Courageous leadership is knowing what's right and then acting on it. For instance, during the Nazi occupation of his country during World War II, King Christian X of Denmark noticed a Nazi flag flying over a Danish public building. He immediately called the German commandant, demanding that the flag be taken down at once. The commandant refused. "Then a soldier will go and take it down," said the king.

"He will be shot," threatened the commandant. "I think not," replied the king, "for I shall be the soldier." Within minutes the flag was taken down. The king was courageous, took his stand, and prevailed.

Engaging leaders don't settle for conditions being forced upon them. As author Marcus Buckingham says, "**The only thing that leaders have in common is leaders break all the rules**." Engaging leaders don't just buy into what everybody else is saying, and they don't follow the beaten path. They are constantly creating their own conditions for success by blazing new trails.

Courage is doing something you are afraid to do. The word "courage" is derived from the medieval French term "corage," meaning heart and spirit.

Howard Schultz, CEO of Starbucks, applied this definition and took his stand when Starbucks wanted to move into a particular international market. Schultz was discouraged by every analysis he read, even after he spent over a half a million dollars on consultants, telling him not to make the move. Furthermore, all his direct reports were against the move. On the advice of one of his gurus, Warren Bennis, he met again with his team, listened to their concerns, answered their questions, and asked for their support. In the end, he had mobilized the support of his management team, and as Bennis had encouraged, he went with his heart, with what he thought was right. He entered the market in question. Schultz stood his ground and, ultimately, was able to score another successful expansion of Starbucks into the international marketplace.

In today's world of boastful leaders in the field of athletics, it seems that balancing courage and humility is a lost art. But the 2006 Winter Olympics offered a shining example for athletes and business leaders, alike.

For 14 days every four years, the Winter Olympics draws thousands of journalists to capture the triumphs of hundreds of athletes on ski runs, bobsled tracks, the ice rinks, and the snowboard courses. Each medal awards ceremony connects with the public's admiration and national pride as athletes representing their home countries take the top step of the awards podium and their country's flag is raised to the strains of the appropriate national anthem.

Without a doubt, everyone loves a winner, but there are also a few winning athletes who use their accomplishments to focus the eyes of the world—if only for a moment—on the needs of the less fortunate. In doing so, they display humility, perhaps, in its purist form. When Joey Cheek, representing the United States in speed skating, won the 500 meter competition, he graciously accepted the gold medal and then made these remarks to the media:

> "I have always felt if I ever do something big like this, I want to be able to give something back. I love what I do; it's

great fun, but honestly, it's a pretty ridiculous thing. I skate around in tights. If you keep it in perspective, I've trained my whole life for this, but it's not that big a deal. But because I skated well, I have a few seconds of microphone time. And I know how news cycles work. Tomorrow there will be another gold medalist. So I can either gush about how wonderful I feel or use it for something.

"So I am donating the entire (winning) sum the USOC gives me ($25,000) to an organization, "Right to Play," that helps refugees in Chad, where there are over 60,000 persons displaced from their homes. I am going to be asking all of the Olympic sponsors if they will match my donation."

Cheek went on to win a second medal, a silver in the 1,000 meters, and elected to give the $15,000 bonus he earned from the Olympic committee to the same cause. In a recap of the 2006 Olympic activities, one commentator mentioned Cheek's $40,000 donation. "It may be that Joey Cheek's humility on the awards podium and the contribution of his medal bonuses to a worthwhile cause may set the stage for more Olympic athletes to do the same in the future."

After the 2006 Olympics concluded, companies around the world had donated a total of $300,000 to match Cheek's contributions.

Humility is not thinking less of ourselves, but thinking of ourselves less, like Joey Cheek did. Engaging leadership, in any venue, is about other people—not us. If we are fortunate enough to build a great team, we will all excel. Staying humble enables us to use our leadership platform to take a stand and conquer much more as a team than we could alone. Our courage must be balanced with humility. Humility is expressed in our actions, not our words.

Taking a stand requires courage to conquer the outside forces and humility to conquer our inside forces.

12

Against All Odds, Persevere

There are no traffic jams along the extra mile.

—ROGER STAUBACH

When I was a senior in high school, I participated in a mock congress with fellow seniors from throughout the state of Florida in a program called Boys' State. It was a defining moment for me. Let me explain.

During the course of the week at the state capital in Tallahassee, we learned about legislative issues, primarily by acting them out and holding mock elections for a variety of political offices. So I figured, "Hey, I'm here only once. Why not just go for it?" So I ran for a lower-level position the second day, but I lost to another student. No problem, I can take rejection. So I tried for a slightly higher office the next day, but I lost again. Now the stakes got higher—more prestigious offices on the line and a bruised ego that needed repair. I tried again but no victory. The next day again—nope! I have to win at some point, right? So one more time I submit my petition, make the rounds, and cast my vote. Votes finally came and I kept my perfect record: 0 wins, 5 losses.

Well, now we were down to the last day of the program and only the highest offices were left to be filled—the governor's cabinet. Here's where the real campaigning kicks in. Pressing flesh, addressing the issues, and making a speech in front of 1,000 of my fellow students (most of whom had won some type of office by now). With five defeats under my belt, there was nothing much left to lose.

With shaking knees and sweating palms, I made my first big speech (thank goodness for lecterns!) as I ran for commissioner of education. I decided to make perseverance one of my issues—it certainly seemed relevant, to me at least. All told, at least I left the week with a one and five record, but the one victory was the one that really counted. Even then, I knew enough to realize that, as Thomas Edison said, **"Genius? Nothing! Sticking to it is the genius! I've failed my way to success."**

Unfortunately, most people fail because they don't stick to things long enough to succeed. Remember the bamboo seed? Sticking to it long enough to win is a key trait of engaging leaders—and their teams. The moments the seeds of our efforts finally "break ground" are so memorable because they often test our faith in ourselves and our teams.

Since we frequently cannot immediately see the tangible results of our leadership, we must trust that doing the right things will yield the desired results. We demonstrate this faith in everyday things, but somehow it seems more challenging with our teams.

For example, I took a lot of pictures of our children this Christmas as they opened their presents. I took some photos with my digital camera. Then I started to feel a bit nostalgic. So I grabbed my old 35-mm camera (call me old fashioned!), put a brand new roll of unexposed film into it, focused on my children, and clicked away. This film was now exposed to the images of my ever-so-happy children. But if I were to open up that camera and look at the film, it wouldn't have looked like anything had happened. I couldn't see one picture that I just took. The film would look totally black.

I know and trust that the images are all there. I just can't see them with my eyes. The film has been exposed to the images of my children. The only problem is that I have not yet developed my film. Now, if I were to take that film to a developer, he would take me into a very dark, dark room, and he would slosh that film around in just the right solutions, and lo and behold, right before my very eyes, a miracle would occur. The images of my children would appear.

> **The signature of mediocrity is constantly changing direction. The signature of excellence is sticking to it.**

They were there all the time. I just couldn't see them until I got the film developed. But the reality is that the moment I snapped the picture that image was imprinted onto that film.

The life of an engaging leader works much the same way. Sometimes, it might feel as though our teams are going through their own "dark room" experience before we finally see the positive results of our efforts. Trust that your efforts will yield the excellence you pursue. The signature of mediocrity is constantly changing direction. The signature of excellence is sticking to it.

Ray Kroc created unparalleled success; most of us are unaware of how he really beat the odds and persevered his way to success.

During his entire life, Ray thrived on discovering just the right idea that would live on well after the man, himself. From a paper cup salesman, to real estate broker, to piano player and, finally, milkshake mixer salesman, he always had an incredible amount of faith in himself!

At the young age of 52, Kroc's biggest idea, McDonald's, was about to emerge. However, Kroc had to muster enough courage in his new idea to mortgage his home and borrow lots of money to get it going. Oh! He wasn't a picture of health, either. He'd been plagued by years with arthritis and diabetes. He lost his bladder and most of his thyroid gland. But he never lost belief in himself. In fact, Ray Kroc was known to say, "The best is ahead of me," according to those who knew him.

Today, the McDonald's brand name is the second-most recognizable name in the world. Not bad for a 52-year-old with health problems, huge debts, and tons of determination!

Ray Kroc was a simple man with a simple plan to achieve huge success. His secret sauce? Against all odds, persevere!

13

Carrying the Torch

Igniting the fire of Passionate Performance for your team is a big responsibility. As a leader, you're the only person who can engage your employees. It's not your boss's responsibility, nor does this task belong to human resources—it's yours. Engaging employees is a personal matter, not an organizational requirement.

Without a doubt, meeting your employees' needs and engaging them is a long-term process, and there are no shortcuts. **You need to mentally prepare for a marathon rather than a sprint**, and there may be some bumps in the road and some detours in your journey.

You may not see the sparks of Passionate Performance until long after the starting gun sounds, just when you're

> **Engaging employees is a personal matter, not an organizational requirement.**

"hitting the wall" of your endurance. That's usually about the time your team experiences that "Aha!" moment and you see positive results for your efforts.

Said one leader, "It's like a 'runner's high'—like hitting the tape at the finish line. Suddenly your team's success appears effortless—you are 'in the zone.'"

But don't expect to hear the cheers of the crowd because only you and your team can fully appreciate the simplicity and the hard work behind your winning ways. And you leave members of your competition in the dust as you cruise past them.

Of course, you will never win the race if you don't *start* the race. A marathoner doesn't start a race thinking about mile 26. A well-trained and confident runner begins the race, thinking about the first mile and then takes it, one step at a time, one water station at a time, one mile at a time.

When you engage your employees, the technique is much the same. With Passionate Performance as your ultimate goal, you have to take one step at a time. **Start the journey by focusing on fulfilling one basic need at a time.**

Time out: Did you know that a lunar voyage is about a half-million miles roundtrip? Now, here's the really interesting part. More energy is spent in the first few seconds and miles of that voyage than in the remaining days and 500,000 miles. Why? Although some of you may have learned this in Space Camp, the gravitational pull of the earth in those first miles is tremendous (probably a lot like pulling kids or grand-kids away from the television on Saturday mornings!). It takes an internal thrust greater than the force of gravity and the resistance of the atmosphere to lift the spacecraft into orbit. But, once it's in orbit, it takes very little power to complete the rest of the trip.

I find this to be a powerful metaphor for describing what it takes to build new, engaging leadership habits. Your first step, of course, is to keep yourself engaged. A truly engaged leader is focused and always ready to envision the next step. Then the leader shares that vision with his or her team.

Staying engaged may be difficult at first because we all have a tendency to let our minds wander. It also may be a little uncomfortable and energy-sapping—and you may even feel some resistance to your own "gravitational pull." But, once you develop a new habit, it becomes comfortable and effortless.

Engaging leaders will tell you that it's well worth the initial discomfort to achieve—and maintain—Passionate Perform-ance. And remember, to get Passionate Performance, you must first give it.

Successful leaders have successful habits. They sacrifice today's pleasures for tomorrow's rewards.

Every journey starts with one step, so let me go the extra mile and suggest your first five steps on your journey to ignite Passionate Performance.

Step 1. *Engaging leaders start with themselves.* They ensure that they are fully engaged before they try to engage their employees. So, if you think your team's achievement is low, examine your own need for achievement. If your team's mastery is lacking, ask yourself what you can do to build your own mastery. If your team's sense of purpose seems heartless, look into the heart of your own purpose. Living a positive example is perhaps the most powerful engagement strategy of all.

Step 2. *Take the Passionate Performance leadership assessment in the appendix.* It will help you identify opportunities for elevating your leadership abilities. Find the two lowest scores and then review the actions you wrote down in the "fulfilling the need" section that corresponds to your two lowest need scores.

Step 3. *Select just one need to work on from your two lowest scores.* Select the one that will ignite the biggest spark of Passionate Performance to help you gain momentum. Here are examples of actions you might take:

- I will look for opportunities to help my team master key skills.

- I will eliminate the primary barrier to achievement by defining clear goals with each employee.

- I will find one reason every day to recognize someone on my team.

- I will ask for suggestions for improvement at every staff meeting.

- I will implement a structured selection process to ensure a good fit between person and position.

- I will review my team's structure to ensure that all team members feel closely connected to their peers and their customers.

- I will ask my employees what changes they can make to be certain we stay focused on our purpose.

Step 4. *Turn the one action you selected into a positive habit.* It takes 28 days of action and reinforcement to create a new habit. So stick to just one action until you're certain you've created a habit that fulfills a basic need for employees. After 28 days of disciplined effort, your new habit should require minimal effort to maintain. It will begin to be the natural way you lead. First we form our habits; then our habits form us.

Step 5. Once your new action has truly become a habit (but not before that time), come back to this book. Identify another need to fulfill, and build another positive habit. Take baby steps to create successes upon which you and your team can build confidence and momentum. Remember, it's a long race.

First we form our habits; then our habits form us.

14

Passing the Torch

In teaching others, we teach ourselves.

—PROVERB

Deepen your own learning and commitment by teaching others about the simplicity and power of igniting Passionate Performance. **Set up a series of brown-bag lunches or dedicate time during your staff meetings to discuss the model and the six employee needs.** During the first meeting, present and discuss the concept of employee engagement and the Passionate Performance model. Then dedicate the next six sessions to explaining each of the needs one at a time. Make sure that you spend plenty of time listening to team members' reactions, thoughts, and ideas. You can even enlist their help in completing some of the Pulse Point exercises from this book.

Start *today* with one simple action. Then follow that up with another. You will be well on your way to meeting your employees' needs. Eventually you will achieve a "runner's high," and you will discover that you have fully engaged the minds and hearts of your employees. Everyone on your team will deliver Passionate Performance every day. **You will win the race and conquer the competition!**

Appendix A

Passionate Performance Leadership Profile

Welcome to the Passionate Performance leadership profile.

Your responses will help you better understand how you can more effectively engage employees' minds and hearts. It should take you only 10 minutes to complete this profile. It contains two brief sections: Intellectual Engagement (Engaging the Mind) and Emotional Engagement (Engaging the Heart).

Important: Predict what the *average* **response of your team would be** if they were completing this profile about you as a leader.

In each of the two sections, please circle the appropriate response (1, 2, 3, 4, or 5) to each question using the following scale:

1 = Strongly disagree   4 = Agree

2 = Disagree   5 = Strongly agree

3 = Neither agree nor disagree

Intellectual Engagement (Engaging the Mind)

Achievement

1. I have no barriers to getting my job done.

① ② ③ ④ ⑤

2. I have sufficient resources available to meet my goals.

① ② ③ ④ ⑤

3. My goals are very clearly defined.

① ② ③ ④ ⑤

4. Decisions are made quickly to help me stay focused on achieving my goals.

① ② ③ ④ ⑤

5. I know how my progress is being measured.

① ② ③ ④ ⑤

6. My fellow team members are committed to doing quality work.

① ② ③ ④ ⑤

Autonomy

1. My team leader involves me in improving work processes.

① ② ③ ④ ⑤

2. I have significant flexibility to enable me to define the best way to get my job done.

① ② ③ ④ ⑤

3. My team leader defines clear boundaries within which I can use my skills and knowledge to make decisions.

① ② ③ ④ ⑤

4. I am expected to provide ideas for improvement.

① ② ③ ④ ⑤

5. I have the authority to implement changes to work processes.

① ② ③ ④ ⑤

6. My opinion really counts.

① ② ③ ④ ⑤

Mastery

1. My job requirements match my natural abilities and interests.

① ② ③ ④ ⑤

2. My skills are put to their "highest and best use" for the organization.

① ② ③ ④ ⑤

3. I never find myself frustrated performing tasks someone else could do that can be eliminated or automated.

① ② ③ ④ ⑤

4. In the past year, I have had an opportunity to develop new job skills.

① ② ③ ④ ⑤

5. My team leader frequently coaches me to help me succeed.

① ② ③ ④ ⑤

6. I have the opportunity to do what I do best every day.

① ② ③ ④ ⑤

Emotional Engagement (Engaging the Heart)

Purpose

1. My team has a clear sense of purpose.

① ② ③ ④ ⑤

2. I know exactly how my role connects to my team's purpose.

① ② ③ ④ ⑤

3. I am very proud to be part of my team.

① ② ③ ④ ⑤

4. I look forward to coming to work each day.

   ① ② ③ ④ ⑤

5. I never have to perform a task that does not directly support my team's purpose.

   ① ② ③ ④ ⑤

6. I feel that my job is important.

   ① ② ③ ④ ⑤

Intimacy

1. I have someone at work who cares about me as a person.

   ① ② ③ ④ ⑤

2. My team is not too large.

   ① ② ③ ④ ⑤

3. I have a best friend at work.

   ① ② ③ ④ ⑤

4. I feel connected to my customers whether they are internal or external.

   ① ② ③ ④ ⑤

5. My team has predictable rituals.

   ① ② ③ ④ ⑤

6. My team's celebrations make me feel connected to my fellow team members.

① ② ③ ④ ⑤

Appreciation

1. In the last two weeks, I have received recognition or praise for doing good work.

① ② ③ ④ ⑤

2. My team leader really knows who I am as a person.

① ② ③ ④ ⑤

3. It is the norm to hear the words "please" and "thank you" on my team.

① ② ③ ④ ⑤

4. My team leader acknowledges my contributions to others who are outside my team.

① ② ③ ④ ⑤

5. My team leader always finds the time to thank me for my efforts.

① ② ③ ④ ⑤

6. I feel like a valuable member of my team.

① ② ③ ④ ⑤

My Passionate Performance
Leadership Scores

Add your scores from each of the preceding sections. Enter them next in the appropriate box in the table below.

	My Score	The Engaging Leader
Intellectual Needs (the Mind)		
Achievement	____	30
Autonomy	____	30
Mastery	____	30
Intellectual Engagement Index (the Mind)	____	90
Emotional Needs (the Heart)		
Purpose	____	30
Intimacy	____	30
Appreciation	____	30
Emotional Engagement Index (the Heart)	____	90
Passionate Performance Index (Overall)	____	180

To compare your scores with up to 10 of your employees' scores about your engagement practices, take the **180-degree version** of this assessment. You can find it at www.Passionate Performance.com.

APPENDIX B

Inspirational Quotes to Help Ignite
Passionate Performance

Since Step 1 on your journey to Passionate Performance is to ensure that *you* are engaged, on the pages that follow are some inspirational quotations for each of the six needs that enable Passionate Performance. You will recall that the six needs are the need for:

- Achievement

- Autonomy

- Mastery

- Purpose

- Intimacy

- Appreciation

ACHIEVEMENT

Happiness lies in the joy of achievement and the thrill of creative effort.

—Franklin D. Roosevelt, American President

Doing the best at this moment puts you in the best place for the next moment.

—Oprah Winfrey, American personality,
actress, and producer

A dream becomes a goal when action is taken toward its achievement.

—Bo Bennett, American businessman

What is the recipe for successful achievement? To my mind, there are just four essential ingredients: choose a career you love, give it the best there is in you, seize your opportunities, and be a member of the team.

—Benjamin F. Fairless, CEO of US Steel

The fear of criticism is the kiss of death in the courtship of achievement.

—Author Unknown

AUTONOMY

You can't always wait for the guys at the top. Every manager at every level in the organization has an opportunity, big or small, to do something. Every manager's got some sphere of autonomy. Don't pass the buck up the line.
— Bob Anderson, American writer

If money is your hope for independence you will never have it. The only real security that a man will have in this world is a reserve of knowledge, experience, and ability.
— Henry Ford, American industrialist

Do we not realize that self respect comes with self reliance?
— Abdul Kalam, President of India, b.1931

If one word can be used to characterize the new career, it is self-reliance... That means you believe in your own competence...because you know you have the skills to sell and you know your own value.
— Barbara Moses, American career-consultant, author

Independence is loyalty to one's best self and principles ...
— Mark Twain, American author and lecturer

MASTERY

If people only knew how hard I work to gain my mastery, it wouldn't seem so wonderful at all.

—Michelangelo Buonarroti, Italian painter and sculptor

To succeed as a team is to hold all of the members accountable for their expertise.

—Mitchell Caplan, CEO, E*Trade Group Inc.

Great ability develops and reveals itself increasingly with every new assignment.

—Baltasar Gracian, Jesuit scholar

Skill and confidence are an unconquered army.

—George Herbert, British poet

It is possible to fly without motors, but not without knowledge and skill.

—Wilbur Wright, American inventor

Only those who have the patience to do simple things perfectly ever acquire the skill to do difficult things easily.

—Author Unknown

PURPOSE

Enjoyment is not a goal; it is a feeling that accompanies important ongoing activity.

—Paul Goodman, American writer

This is the true joy in life—being used for a purpose recognized by yourself as a mighty one....

—George Bernard Shaw, British playwright

Thoughts lead on to purposes; purposes go forth in action; actions form habits; habits decide character; and character fixes our destiny.

—Tryon Edwards, American theologian

Concern should drive us into action and not into depression.

—Author Unknown

Lack of something to feel important about is almost the greatest tragedy a man may have.

—Arthur E. Morgan, American educator
and college president

INTIMACY

Intimacy is being seen and known as the person you truly are.
— Amy Bloom, American psychotherapist

Understanding is a two-way street.
— Eleanor Roosevelt, American First Lady

"You can't love a crowd the same way you can love a person. And a crowd can't love you the way a single person can love you. Intimacy doesn't scale. Not really. Intimacy is a one-on-one phenomenon."
— Hugh Macleod, British advertising executive

A friendship founded on business is better than a business founded on friendship.
— John D. Rockefeller Jr., American industrialist

The only way to make a man trustworthy is to trust him.
— Henry Stimson, American Secretary of War

APPRECIATION

Appreciation can make a day, even change a life. Your willingness to put it into words is all that is necessary.
> —Margaret Cousins, American author

In my wide association in life ... I have yet to find the man ... who did not do better work and put forth greater effort under a spirit of approval than he would ever do under a spirit of criticism.
> —Charles M. Schwab, American businessman

Appreciation is the highest form of prayer, for it acknowledges the presence of good wherever you shine the light of your thankful thoughts.
> —Alan Cohen, American author

The greatest humiliation in life is to work hard on something from which you expect great appreciation, and then fail to get it.
> —Edgar Watson Howe, American editor

By appreciation, we make excellence in others our own property.
> —Voltaire, French playwright and poet

APPENDIX C

Checklist for Engaging Meetings

Meetings are often a primary source of disengagement, primarily because of lack of preparation. The wrong people are present or absent, goals are unclear, roles are confused, the meeting ends late, and so on. These dynamics result in feelings of frustration, confusion, disrespect for one's time—all seeds of disengagement.

Here is a simple checklist to help ensure engaging meetings. Take just a few minutes to answer these questions and you will be rewarded with passionate performance during and after your meetings.

WHY? (Purpose)

- Why is a meeting necessary?

- Can your goal be accomplished using a different medium? (Obtain progress reports in writing or through one-on-one meetings.)

- What's the purpose of the meeting—to inform, influence, create, or decide?

WHAT? (Agenda)

- Which topics must be covered?

- What information is needed in advance?

WHO? (Team Members)

- Who really must be present in order to achieve the meeting's purpose? (no more, no less)

- Are the necessary skills and departments represented?

WHEN? (Timing)

- Have I kept the meeting under one hour? (If not, split it into two meetings.)

- Is it scheduled at a reasonable time? (Before lunch and at the end of the day are the worst times.)

WHERE? (Location)

- Does the room comfortably accommodate the participants?

- Does the set-up/configuration facilitate discussion?

- What equipment is needed (flip chart, audiovisual, refreshments, and so on)?

HOW? (Group Process)

- What roles will be assigned (scribe, timer, facilitator)?

- How will input be solicited from each participant?

- How will decisions be made (by group consensus)?

- What follow-up actions will be taken, by whom, and when?

APPENDIX D

Passionate Performance Killers

Words reflect our commitments to act. **Our words tell the truth**. Whether we have a long conversation with a friend, place an order at a restaurant, or discuss expectations with a team member, every word makes a difference. The results of our interactions are rarely neutral; they are almost always positive or negative. Ask yourself, "Do my words reflect a commitment to passionate performance?"

Words are the seeds of commitment. We plant the seeds with each movement of our lips. Once they are spoken, our words either grow in the form of an immediate response or they take time to germinate. Whether the result becomes apparent sooner or later, we cannot speak words of failure and defeat and expect a life of success and victory.

So a leader's words can help grow a team's engagement and discretionary effort. They can also plant the seeds for disengagement. Avoid these phrases to help keep your team on the fast track to passionate performance!

- That's' a good idea, but ...

- It's against company policy.

- All right in theory, but ...

- Well, let's be practical.

- That costs too much.

- Don't start anything yet.

- It's not part of your job.

- Let's sit on it for a while.

- That's not our problem.

- It's too hard to administer.

- We have been doing it this way for a long time and it works.

- If it ain't broken, let's not fix it.

- Why hasn't someone suggested it before if it's a good idea?

- We've never done it that way.

- Who else has tried it?

APPENDIX E

Leading on Purpose

My Team's Purpose: _____

_____

_____

_____

_____

_____

_____

_____

_____

_____

_____

_____

My Daily Tasks	Impact on My Team's Purpose (High, Medium, or Low)
1.	
2.	
3.	
4.	
5.	
6.	
7.	
8.	
9.	
10.	

Total number of tasks rated:

High = _____   Medium = _____   Low = _____

NOTES

Introduction

1. http://www.hoover.org/research/factsonpolicy/facts/4931661.html, article, "Facts on Policy," December 19, 2006.
2. http://www.govleaders.org/gallup_article_getting_personal.htm.
3. http://www.govleaders.org/gallup_article_getting_personal.htm.
4. http://www.hewittassociates.com/Intl/NA/enUS/ KnowledgeCenter/ArticlesReports/ArticleDetail.aspx?cid=3680 &tid=47.
5. http://www.shrm.org/foundation.
6. http://www.gruntledemployees.com/gruntled_employees/client_ service/index.html.
7. www.snopes.com/business/consumer/nordstrom.asp.
8. Thomas J. Peters and Robert H. Waterman, *In Search of Excellence: Lessons from America's Best-Run Companies*, New York: Collins Business Essentials, 2004.

Chapter 1

9. Peter Drucker, *Management Challenges for the 21st Century*, New York, HarperBusiness, 2001.
10. http://gmj.gallup.com/content/28867/Many-Employees-Would-Fire-Their-Boss.aspx.

11. http://gmj.gallup.com/content/14545/Gallup-Study-Unhappy-Workers-Unhealthy-Too.aspx

12. Lorraine Grubbs-West, *Lessons in Loyalty: How Southwest Airlines Does It—An Insider's View*, Dallas: CornerStone Leadership Institute, 2005, pp. 24-26.

13. http://money.cnn.com/galleries/2007/fortune/0701/gallery. Google_perks/.

14. http://www.strategy-business.com/press/16635507/04410.

Chapter 2

15. http://gmj.gallup.com/content/28867/Many-Employees-Would-Fire-Their-Boss.aspx.

16. http://gmj.gallup.com/content/829/Gallup-Study-Finds-Many-Employees-Doubt-Ethics-Corporate-Leaders.aspx.

Chapter 4

17. http://truettcathy.com/about_recipe.asp.

18. http://truettcathy.com/about_recipe.asp.

19. http://www.agilent.com/about/companyinfo/agilentfactbook.pdf, pp. 4–5.

20. http://www.answers.com/topic/nordstrom-inc?cat=biz-fin.

Part II (Opening Section)

21. Lorraine Grubbs-West, *Lessons in Loyalty: How Southwest Airlines Does It-An Insider's View* Dallas: CornerStone Leadership Institute, 2005, pp. 50–51.

22. http://ideas.wordpress.com/2006/01/25/why-do-talented-employees-leave-companies.

Chapter 5

23. http://phx.corporate-ir.net/phoenix.zhtml?c=102601&p=irol-newsArticle_Print&ID=390867&highlight=.

Chapter 8

24. http://www.fastcompany.com/magazine/81/immelt.html.

25. http://www.google.com/support/jobs/bin/static.py?page=about.html&about=top10.

26. http://www.wegmans.com/webapp/wcs/stores/servlet/About UsView?storeId=10052&catalogId=10002&langId=-1/.

Chapter 9

27. http://www.google.com/support/jobs/bin/static.py?page=about.html.

28. Alice Adams, "Salute to Nurses," *The Houston Chronicle*, May 2006.

29. http://gmj.gallup.com/content/25369/Praise-Praising-Your-Employees.aspx.

Chapter 10

30. http://www.vistage.com/featured/four-steps-to-keep-your-employees-motivated-and-turnover-low.html.

31. http://gmj.gallup.com/content/12289/New-Book-Shows-How-Positivity-Increases-Productivity.aspx.

32. http://www.harrisinteractive.com.

33. Ferdinand F. Fournies, *Why Employees Don't Do What They Are Supposed to . . . and What to Do about It*, New York: McGraw-Hill, 1999).

INDEX

ABOUT THE AUTHOR

Lee J. Colan, PhD, is a leadership expert, adviser, and an energizing speaker. He is passionate about delivering simple, powerful tools that leaders can put to work right away. Lee's cut-through-the-clutter insights appear regularly in a wide range of print and online media. He is also a frequent presenter at corporate meetings. Virtually every Fortune 500 company, and many smaller companies as well, has experienced the positive impact of Lee's practical approach.

To learn more about his practical tools and to access *free* leadership resources, visit www.theLgroup.com or call 972-250-9989.

6 WAYS

to Ignite *Passionate Performance* in Your Organization!

1. Keynote Presentation

Invite author Lee J. Colan to ignite your organization and share insights to help your managers become more engaging leaders.

2. Workshop

Facilitated by the author or a certified facilitator, this three- or six-hour workshop delivers relevant examples and practical tools that can be applied immediately. Participants will create personal action plans to become more engaging leaders.

3. PowerPoint® Presentation

Introduce and reinforce the Passionate Performance concepts and strategies to your team with this professionally designed presentation. Use the presentation for staff meetings, brown-bag lunches, or as a follow-up development tool. 48 slides plus 4 bonus tools.

4. At-a-Glance Reminder Cards

These attractively designed, quick-reference cards summarize the key strategies for engaging your team members to boost their discretionary effort. Perfect for all leaders to have at their fingertips! 5-inch × 7-inch cards. Package of 10.

5. Facilitator's Training Kit

Help your organization build a competitive advantage with this just-add-water training kit based on the bestselling book.

This workshop helps your leaders fully engage their employees and increase their team's discretionary efforts. The flex agenda enables you to adjust to meet your needs and desired areas of focus. Includes facilitator guide in a 3-ring binder, participant guide, slide show, and at-a-glance reminder card.

6. The 180-Degree Passionate Performance Online Leadership Assessment

This confidential, online profile assesses your team's intellectual and emotional engagement. The Passionate Performance profile is easy to use and provides you with valuable insights into the six critical employee needs. You receive a 20+ page, personalized profile comparing your self-assessment with assessments from up to 10 of your employees.

THE **L** GROUP
Leadership at every level.

Consulting: Our top-notch consultants deliver cut-through-the-clutter insights that drive results for your team.

Executive Coaching: Our advisors help executives boost team and personal performance.

Speaking: Engage your team with passionate delivery and equip them with practical tools.

Resources: Rapid-read books, multi-media training tools and leadership assessments.

Training: Rely on our certified facilitators (English or Spanish speaking) or use our just-add-water training kits for internal delivery.

theLgroup.com   972.250.9989